Continuous Improvement and Measurement for Total Quality:

A Team-Based Approach

Dennis C. Kinlaw, Ed.D.

San Diego • Toronto • Amsterdam • Sydney

in association with

Homewood, Illinois

Copyright © 1992 by Pfeiffer & Company
ISBN 1-55623-778-2
Library of Congress Catalog Card Number: 91-42840

Printed in the United States of America.

Library of Congress Cataloging-in-Publication Data
Kinlaw, Dennis C.
    Continuous improvement and measurement for total quality: a team-based approach / Dennis C. Kinlaw
    p. cm.
    Includes bibliographical references and index.
    ISBN 1-55623-778-2 (hardback : acid free)
    1. Total quality management. 2. Quality control. 3. Work groups.
    4. Quality circles. I. Title.
    HD62.15.K56 1992   91-42840
    658.5'62—dc20   CIP

This book is printed on acid-free, recycled stock that meets or exceeds the minimum GPO and EPA specifications for recycled paper.

Dedication

For Alexander, the living proof
of continuous improvement

Preface

It has taken a long time for the concept of total quality management (TQM) to develop in the United States, although that is where it began. Its historical roots go back at least as far as the 1900s and Walter A. Shewhart. Shewhart was a physicist with Bell Telephone Laboratories; he determined that in any work process there would be natural variation. He reached the conclusion that it would be desirable and possible to set limits on the natural variation of any process, so that fluctuations within these limits could be explained by chance causes, but any variation outside these limits would indicate a change in the underlying process. In 1931, he published his conclusions in the book, *The Economic Control of Quality of Manufactured Product.*

It took over fifty years for Shewhart's work to find general acceptance and application in the United States. His work made a circuitous and costly detour (at least for the United States) via Japan.

In 1947, Kenichi Koyanagi formed the Japanese Union of Scientists and Engineers (JUSE). Through JUSE, W. Edwards Deming, an American disciple of Shewhart, was invited to Japan to present a series of lectures to the leaders of Japanese industry on the statistical approach to managing quality. Deming was followed by Joseph M. Juran, who presented seminars on the system of total quality management in organizations. Within the unbelievably short time of ten years, Japan was setting the standards of quality in the manufacture of steel and in the production of automobiles and electronics.

The work of Shewhart finally was reintroduced to America (via Japan and through Deming) for general consumption in 1981. In that year, Deming appeared on a documentary television program entitled, "If Japan Can, Why Can't We?" As a result, he was asked by such major organizations as General Motors and Ford to give seminars to company executives on the management of total quality.

It has been through the work of Deming (1981, 1982, 1985), his recent converts, and people like Joseph M. Juran (1964, 1986), Kaoru Ishikawa (1985), Philip B. Crosby (1979, 1984), and Armand V. Feigenbaum (1983) that the spotlight has been placed on quality in most companies and that TQM has become so pervasive a movement throughout America.

The growth of the TQM movement has paralleled the development of an extensive and rich literature. Guides, anthologies, programmatic descriptions, how-to books, declarations about the TQM imperative, training packages, and testimonies about successes have been published at an ever-increasing rate. In this highly varied and expanding field of publications, there is an extremely diverse and prolific set of contributors. Executives, managers, consultants, trainers, free-lance writers, and academics all have had a great deal to say from a multitude of perspectives.

So much now has been written by so many on the continuous improvement of quality that one must ask what still needs to be said and whether there is justification for another book on the subject. I have found this question troublesome as I have presumed to offer a book about the improvement and measurement of quality.

I have written this book, in the first place, to affirm what I have not seen so clearly and unambiguously stated elsewhere. It is that *team development must precede all other kinds of improvement initiatives and that teams, more than executive leadership, cultural change, TQM training, or any other strategy, account for most major improvements in organizations.* Team development must be strategically placed at the very center of TQM and must form the hub around which all other elements of TQM (customer satisfaction, supplier performance, measurement and assessment, and so on) must revolve.

My second reason for writing this book is based on the observation that people in organizations do not serve on only one team; typically, they serve concurrently on many kinds of teams.

Teams exist whenever and wherever two or more people join forces to do work. During any given work day, people may work as members of several formal and informal teams. They will be linked informally with colleagues, suppliers, and customers and will team up to resolve a variety of problems and make a number of decisions. They also will serve as members of some work team or management team. In addition, they may be members of a variety of special teams, such as interface teams, processes-improvement teams, quality-action teams, tiger teams, committees, and councils.

The call for continuous improvement can create a variety of responses. If it is not accompanied and supported by a clear description of what people are expected to do, the call for continuous improvement can create an enormous amount of confusion, false starts, and wasted effort.

People at work need a model of continuous improvement that they can generalize and apply to all the many different kinds of teams on which they serve. They need a model that can be translated readily into a plan of action for continuous improvement.

My second reason for writing this book is, therefore, to provide a model of continuous improvement that has been designed specifically for teams and which people can apply to any sort of team on which they may serve.

Teams are the primary units of performance in organizations. They are, inevitably, the most direct sources of continuous improvement. This book affirms teams as this source and provides them with the necessary guidance and the necessary tools to act.

This book also affirms that teams do not need to wait for permission to improve themselves and their organizations. They need only act. When they act, however, they need to make data-based decisions and to construct improvement projects whose results can be measured. My hope is that this book will encourage them to do so.

Table of Contents

Introduction

$\mathbf{T}$he hottest topic and most pervasive issue in organizations today is quality—and its various extensions, such as improvement and competitiveness. I know of no large organization in the United States that has not launched a formal, total-quality initiative or (to use the most current phrase) a total quality management (TQM) program. I know of very few employees who are not aware of TQM, although in their own companies they may use alternative phrases, such as the quality advantage, quality improvement, quality systems, quality action, quality leadership, and the like.

COMMON CHARACTERISTICS OF TQM

The TQM initiatives that have produced significant successes and that have begun to realize the goal of continuous improvement all have in common one very obvious and dominant characteristic. They depend on teamwork as the major strategy and underlying framework of TQM. Over and over again, we find that TQM is a team-centered and team-driven activity (Kinlaw, 1991).

Although the team-centered characteristic is the most dominant and obvious one of all TQM initiatives, there are others. Among these are:

- **Customer Satisfaction**. The customer (internal and external) is unambiguously established as the final arbiter of quality. All final organizational results, such as reputation, market share, and profit are seen as secondary outcomes of customer satisfaction.

- **Continuous Improvement**. Continuous improvement of every aspect of work and business is viewed as everyone's responsibility. No practice, policy, tool, system, service, or product is exempt from scrutiny and change. Each person is seen as a potential source of new ideas and innovation.

- **Assessment and Measurement**. In TQM, customer satisfaction and continuous improvement are shown and proved by *measurement*. Measurement and the display of performance data on run charts, histograms, and control charts are expected.

- **Supplier Performance**. The continual improvement of total quality is impossible without input from internal and external suppliers that is on time and fully fit to use. To achieve continual improvement of total quality, teams and organizations assume responsibility *with* their suppliers to improve their suppliers' performance.

- **Environmental Support**. Executives and leaders at all organizational levels demonstrate total and unflagging support for TQM. These leaders ensure that there is a plan to shape the TQM initiative and that the resources are available to support the initiative over the long term.

- **Systems Support**. Personnel systems are modified and aligned to support TQM. Performance appraisal, if done at all, becomes focused on work teams. Awards recognize team achievement more than individual achievement. Hiring involves team decisions. Job descriptions reflect core responsibilities for quality and continuous improvement.

- **Training**. TQM requires new skills for developing and leading teams, planning and managing TQM, satisfying and responding to customers, structured problem solving, process analysis and simplification, statistical process control, and measurement.

The Team-Centered Model for TQM (Figure I-1) displays these TQM characteristics and depicts their interdependence on team development and performance.

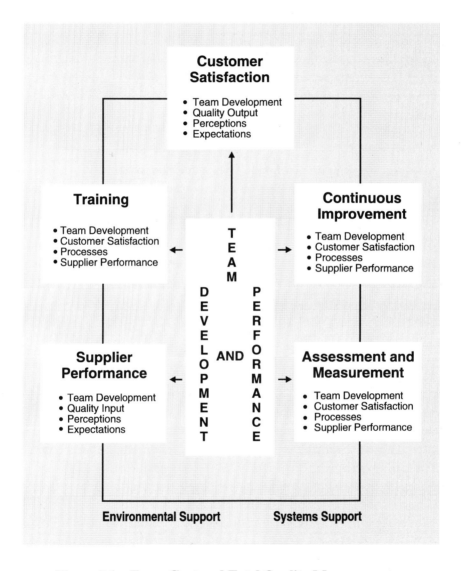

Figure I-1. Team-Centered Total Quality Management

The training element in the Team-Centered Model for TQM supports all the other elements. Customer satisfaction, continuous improvement, measurement, and (above all) team development all have created their own special requirements for training materials and programs. Currently, there is a prodigious output of descriptive materials about TQM, tools for planning and managing total quality, training packages on TQM methods and techniques, and guidelines for organizing and developing teams.

There are, of course, many tools that people need in order to undertake improvement projects in a careful and systematic way. They need problem-solving tools, such as flow-charts and cause-and-effect diagrams. They need to know how to create run charts, histograms, and Pareto charts. They need statistical tools to control their systems. They need to know how to plan and collect data and how to use check sheets.

But beyond all these particular tools, the leaders and members of teams need a picture or overview of the *total* process of continuous improvement and measurement. They need a way to visualize the interconnectedness of all the improvements that they might make. They need a framework and a set of common symbols that they can use to communicate their thoughts and plans about improvement. In short, they need an improvement and measurement model and they need guidance in using such a model. This book describes such a model and provides such guidance.

The information in this book centers around a Model for Continuous Improvement and Measurement (Figure 2-1) and is largely an explication of that model. The model has grown out of my practical experience. It has proven successful in such widely dissimilar organizations as mental-health groups and engineering firms. It provides an explicit answer to the question that people have when they first become committed to TQM: "What do I do next?" The model also leads people to recognize that the question must be rephrased from, "What do *I* do next?" to "What do *we* do next?"

The model has been created for teams of every kind and at every organizational level. It has been tested with teams. It has, in truth, been designed by teams. My underlying assumption is that TQM and continuous improvement are team-centered and team-driven (Kinlaw, 1991). The model becomes a real tool only when it is taken up by any of the many kinds of teams that make TQM a reality: management teams, work teams, project teams, special problem- solving teams, and others.

Throughout this book, I will refer to various TQM tools, such as histograms, run charts, and control charts. I also will use common statistical terms, such as distribution, average, and variation. This is, however, neither a book on TQM tools nor one on statistics. It is a book about designing projects for continuous improvement.

I have included additional information in the Appendix about various TQM tools. The reader is strongly encouraged to consult any of the many excellent books already available on TQM tools and statistics for additional help.

A detailed overview of the Model for Continuous Improvement and Measurement is provided in Chapter 2. Each element in the model is further elaborated in the subsequent chapters.

PURPOSES OF THE BOOK

This book has been written for anyone who has a serious and practical interest in TQM and continuous improvement, with a primary focus on teams. I believe that leaders and members of every kind of organizational team (e.g., management teams, work teams, project teams, TQM teams) who are embarking on the endless journey of continuous improvement will find immediate help here. I also expect that TQM specialists, trainers, and consultants will discover this book to be a useful resource in their professional work. The specific kinds of help that the book provides are:

- A model for gaining a practical and integrated under-standing of continuous improvement;
- A model for planning and undertaking improvement and measurement projects;

- Tools for improving and measuring levels of team development;
- Tools for improving and measuring output and customer satisfaction;
- Tools for improving and measuring the performance of work processes; and
- Tools for improving and measuring input and the performance of suppliers.

This book has been designed for use in several ways:

- For teams and team members as they plan and initiate continuous improvement;
- As a guide for managers, supervisors, and other key people who are responsible for managing continuous improvement and measurement;
- As a guide for staff members and other people who have some special organizational responsibility for TQM;
- As a conceptual framework for consultants and trainers to use to help others to initiate and manage continuous improvement and measurement; and
- As an adjunct resource for people who are involved in any aspect of continuous improvement and measurement.

Chapter  1

The Meaning of Improvement and Measurement

$\mathbf{T}$his book is about improvement and measurement. It is important to recognize the special meaning that these terms have throughout this book and to know how they are interrelated and interdependent. Throughout this book, improvement and measurement are intended to convey the following:

- Improvement and measurement always must be kept together as elements in a unified concept;
- Improvement and measurement are a function of team involvement and commitment;
- Improvement has less to do with individuals and their motivation to work than it has to do with other factors; and
- Improvement can play a major role in the life of teams and organizations only when it becomes continuous.

KEEPING IMPROVEMENT AND MEASUREMENT TOGETHER

1. The first, and most obvious, reason for coupling improvement with measurement is that we cannot know that we have improved the quality of performance until we have measured it. It may, of course, be possible to think of improvement in certain ways and in contexts that do not require measurement. We may, for example, appropriately

conclude that we feel better, that we are more optimistic, or that our personal relationships are improving without using some type of measurement to gauge these changes. But to judge that some work process is more efficient, or that some product is more error free, or that a customer is more satisfied with our services, we cannot rely solely on feelings. Such a judgment requires the periodic measurement of one or more quality indicators over time. Improvement and measurement must be kept together because improvement in the quality of performance cannot be planned or verified unless it is measured. For purposes of guiding decisions, improvement does not exist (in any useful way) until it is measured.

2. Another reason that improvement and measurement must be kept together is to keep ourselves clearly focused on concrete opportunities. If we encourage improvement without measurement, we encourage ourselves and others to identify improvement targets that may be vague, grandiose, or outside our field of influence and control. An axiom for designing improvement projects should be, "If you can't measure it, don't do it."

3. Keeping improvement and measurement together also keeps us from taking a random approach to improvement. This sort of randomness is what we often see when executives and managers decide to do things such as change the structures and relationships of their organization without having first established baseline performance variables that can be tracked to show that the new state of affairs is better than the former. Random change is not the same as improvement. Random change usually exists when organizations move people around, change policies and practices, modify job descriptions and titles, or alter work systems. The improvement of quality is possible only when data (rather than whim or bias) are the basis for making decisions.

4. Improvement should be celebrated. It is difficult to celebrate the achievement of a nonspecific improvement, i.e., one that has not been measured. One of the great values in measurement that often is overlooked is that it permits us to acknowledge achievement in a clear and unambiguous way.

5. Measurement creates a higher degree of involvement of people in the goals and processes of improvement. Measurement provides the feedback that helps people to take more active roles in improvement and to take more direct responsibility for it. When improvement goals are vague and progress goes unmonitored, we encourage people to remain on the sidelines and to avoid ownership.

6. A final reason for keeping improvement and measurement linked is to keep improvement from being confused with the more general strategies of managing change and the resistances to change. Improvement, when initiated by teams and clearly measured and documented, will be viewed as an opportunity. People resist change out of fear and ignorance. People do not fear improvement. They fear any cost in time and effort that does not lead to their growth or sense of personal achievement. They fear changes that are not concrete. They do not fear being rewarded and recognized. Measured improvement provides people with knowledge and certainty and provides the organization with a concrete basis for acknowledging people's achievements.

People in organizations often are wary of change, with good reason. Few of the changes that they have suffered through in their organizations have turned out to be improvements. Many have just been disruptions. How often have people been told that an organizational "restructuring" was going to result in greater efficiency, effectiveness, and communication, but the result was only a new wire diagram and an organization with the same old values and the same leadership style? How often have performance-appraisal systems been initiated or reformed in order to "improve the capacity of supervisors to manage the performance of their subordinates" when the result only was more paperwork? How often have the latest fads, such as zero-based budgeting, zero defects, management by objectives, etc., been forced on people with great fanfare when the results merely were different slogans, more controls, and more bureaucracy?

IMPROVEMENT AS A FUNCTION OF TEAM INVOLVEMENT AND COMMITMENT

Improvement in the quality of performance often is associated with causes such as:

- the leadership styles of supervisors, managers, and executives;
- the activities of entrepreneurs;
- the flexibility of organizations and their capacities to change;
- the aggressive acquisition of new technology;
- the planning processes of organizations;
- the control systems in organizations;
- the visions of executives; and
- the cultures of organizations.

All these causes and more are, no doubt, in some way associated with improvement. None of them, however, reflect the perspective of this book and the experience of its author. None capture the day-to-day reality of improvement. All reflect one or both of the following assumptions: (a) improvement largely is a result of individual initiative (or the collective initiatives of individuals); and (b) improvement requires some sort of large-scale change in the total organization. I do not deny that improvement may occur through individual effort and that it may result from some sweeping organizational change. No one can question the importance of executive leadership to focus a total organization on improvement. Nevertheless, *improvement, however it is conceived, planned, or initiated, almost invariably comes down to the cooperative actions of teams of people.*

I certainly do not discount the need for large-scale and long-term changes. Nor do I question the need for many organizations to undertake major overhauls of their planning processes, their leadership styles, and their total cultures. But my interest in improvement has had a different and more modest focus. I have been interested in improvement as an immediate possibility—one that does not have to wait for large-scale reforms in organizations. This also reflects my belief that improvement in organizations rarely takes place in an orderly, sequential, top-down process. It certainly is helped along by executive commitment and senior-management attention. Nonetheless, improvement often proceeds along a helter-skelter route or along a variety of parallel routes that become integrated only after the passage of time.

The early stages in an organization's startup of TQM can serve as an example. When organizations begin to initiate TQM, some managers become committed and involved easily, and others resist and drag their feet; some employees receive training and start using their new TQM skills before others; and some work teams quickly assimilate the new emphasis on customer satisfaction, while others find the going slow.

I have observed that when work teams are introduced to the principles and key elements of TQM (shown in Figure I-1), many of them immediately begin to plan and initiate very significant improvement projects without waiting for additional information or training. Over the years, through my experience with many different improvement strategies, I have come to believe several related axioms about improvement. These axioms form the perspective about improvement that is reflected in this book. They are:

1. Teams (in their many shapes and forms) are the most significant units of production.
2. It follows from the first axiom that teams are potentially able to improve the quality of performance significantly.

3. All teams enjoy at least some degree of autonomy to act.

4. It follows from the first three axioms that teams can make significant improvements whenever they make the decision to improve some aspect of their performance.

The second distinctive characteristic of my point of view about improvement and measurement is that improvement and measurement are a function of team involvement and commitment. A corollary is that the measurement of improvement always refers to the measurement of the performance of teams and what they improve. Throughout this book, measurement always refers to the measurement of the performance of systems and teams, never to the measurement of the performance of individuals.

IMPROVEMENT HAS LESS TO DO WITH MOTIVATION THAN WITH OTHER FACTORS

Another characteristic of the meaning that I give to improvement is that improvement has less to do with individuals and their motivation to work than it has to do with other factors. Of course, the value of individual effort cannot be denied; but individual effort plays a secondary role in the kinds and levels of improvement in quality that organizations need. There are two reasons for this: (a) we already have a motivated work force, and the great majority of people fully intend to do their best (Yankelovich & Immerwahr, 1983); and (b) work processes or systems present the major opportunities for improvement; therefore, getting people to work harder in poor systems will produce minimum improvement.

When organizational performance shows significant improvement, this improvement is not the sum of individual performances. It is first of all the result of improved processes. It also is the synergetic result of team performance. The capacities and limits of individuals are transcended by collecting individuals into teams, and the capacities and limits of organizations are transcended by integrating teams into a larger whole.

Significant improvements in the quality of products, services, and customer satisfaction result from improvements in work processes. These work processes are not under the control of any one person. They are under the control of a number of people who often function in one kind of organizational team or another, e.g., work teams, interface teams, project teams, management teams, and the like. Individuals can improve customer satisfaction and work processes only through teamwork and with the help and cooperation of their fellow work-team members.

We cannot obtain significant improvement by strengthening the motivation of individuals or by getting people to work harder. If we focus on individuals at all, it should be to help them to develop the skills to be superior team players.

There is one more distinctive characteristic in the meaning that I give to improvement and its measurement. Improvement must be continuous to be real.

IMPROVEMENT MUST BE CONTINUOUS

Until improvement is continuous, it will never be viewed as a regular and routine part of performance. Until it is viewed as the norm, improvement will be a response to organizational "pain."

Responding to pain, i.e., taking care of immediate problems, is, of course, absolutely essential. But if teams and organizations stay stuck at this level, they will not institutionalize continuous improvement.

Continuous improvement means undertaking improvement projects that range from fixing things that fail to creating new processes, services, and products. It means solving a customer's immediate problem and it means preventing the same problem (or class of problems) from happening again. Figure 1-1 suggests that there are at least five general strategies for improvement. These strategies exist on a continuum from being reactive to being proactive.

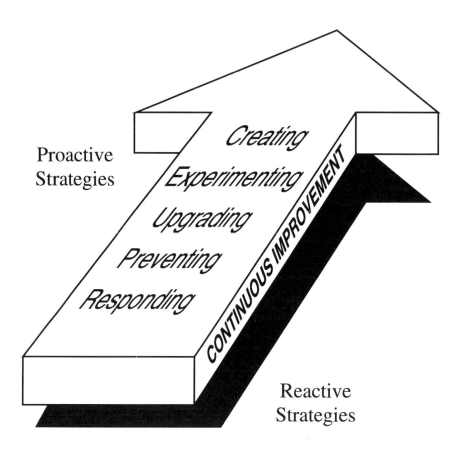

Figure 1-1. Improvement Strategies

Continuous Improvement and Measurement for Total Quality

Beginning at the reactive end of the continuum, the various strategies are:

- **Responding** to an immediate problem. This strategy includes actions such as correcting errors in a procurement request, repairing broken product elements, taking care of customer complaints, and resolving conflict between team members.

- **Preventing** the occurrence or recurrence of a problem. This strategy for improvement focuses on actions such as preventing customer dissatisfaction by inspecting products and not shipping substandard ones, by preventing the failure of a machine through maintenance, by changing a manufacturing process to reduce loss of time in transport, or by preventing errors in a procurement request by internal editing and review.

- **Upgrading** machines, methods, and techniques. Work processes and their results often can be improved by replacing machines with new and better ones, by automating some or all of a work process, or by introducing a job aid or new tool.

- **Experimenting** to improve an operation or work process. This strategy for improvement means designing to test the impact of a modification in sequence, timing, equipment, materials, etc., in a process that is under control and then measuring the results of the modification. Examples are changing the composition of a solution for bleaching textiles and eliminating a point of inspection in a work process and then measuring changes in quality.

- **Creating** a new opportunity. The most proactive strategy for improvement includes such things as the active search to anticipate the developing needs of a customer and the introduction of products or services to meet these needs, the total elimination of outmoded work processes, and breaking out of the many limits to inquiry and improvement that typically exist (see Chapter 8). Examples are the elimination of product inspection, the creation of self-managed work teams, the concurrent design of a product and the process by which to make it (concurrent engineering), and the elimination of inventory.

It is most likely that none of the strategies ever exist in a pure form. They often exist together, and it is often the case that the use of one strategy will lead to another. Taken together, these strategies describe the level of activity that must be going on all the time in order to ensure that improvement is continuous.

Anything other than continuous improvement becomes as ludicrous as holding a "customer appreciation day." Customer appreciation counts only when it becomes embedded in every transaction with the customers.

Measurement is a key to institutionalizing continuous improvement. *We cannot possibly commit to continuous improvement if we collect data only when we have a problem, rather than collecting data as a way of doing business.* It is by having current data about levels of customer satisfaction, about the performance of our work processes, and about the quality of what our suppliers deliver that we can achieve continuous improvement.

In summary, the special meaning that I give to improvement and measurement is as follows:

- Improvement and measurement always must be linked together as elements in a unified concept;

- Improvement and measurement are functions of team involvement and commitment;

- Improvement has little or nothing to do with individuals and their motivation to work; and

- Improvement can play a major role in the life of teams and organizations only when it becomes continuous.

Chapter 2

A Model for Continuous Improvement and Measurement

The basic tool that teams must have in order to undertake the process of continuous improvement is a common understanding of what they are going to do and how they will proceed. Team members must be able to think, conceptualize, and plan together. They need a model by which they can identify specific targets for improvement and can design projects to reach these targets. The purpose of this chapter is to provide such a model.

The Model for Continuous Improvement and Measurement (Figure 2-1) is a practical and tested model that can provide teams with a common framework for continuous improvement. The model can serve a variety of purposes. It can help teams to:

- develop an overview of the many opportunities that they have for continuous improvement;
- consider how improvement and measurement initiatives are connected and interact with one another; and
- develop a comprehensive approach to improvement and measurement.

To use the model, it is necessary to: (a) understand the meaning of each of the model's components, and (b) understand how each of the components is related to the others.

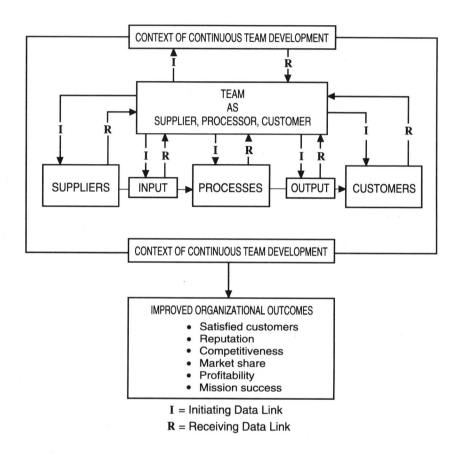

Figure 2-1. A Model for Continuous Improvement and Measurement

OVERVIEW OF THE MODEL

The Model for Continuous Improvement and Measurement suggests the following logic: *Improved organizational outcomes* in the areas of satisfied external customers, reputation, competitiveness, market share, profitability, and mission success are created through the many projects of continuous improvement undertaken by teams in the areas of team development, customer satisfaction, work processes, and supplier performance.

The Model for Continuous Improvement and Measurement provides the structure for this book. It has the following components:

- context of continuous team development,
- roles (team as supplier, processor, and customer),
- input and output connecting links, and
- data links.

Of course, not all organizational-improvement outcomes derive directly from teams and the results of their continuous-improvement initiatives. Executive decisions, changes in technology, pure chance, and many other factors stimulate and initiate improvement. However, because teams are the primary units of production, they also are the primary sources of continuous improvement.

Because teams are the primary sources of continuous improvement, team development is the basic strategy for continuous improvement. It is the daily success that teams have in developing themselves that is the foundation for all other improvements. It is the multitude of improvements that teams make in customer satisfaction, work processes, and supplier performance that, taken in aggregate, account for any organization's capacity to institutionalize and sustain the total enterprise of continuous improvement.

Context of Continuous Team Development

The most distinctive characteristic of the model is that it places all activities, projects, and other continuous-improvement initiatives within the context of team development. The other components of the model, such as the roles of supplier, processor, and customer are found in most models that describe the processes of improvement, but the context of team development is omitted from such models.

In the model, the context of team development surrounds the entire primary system of continuous improvement. The idea is that team development affects the ways in which teams function in their roles of suppliers, processors, and customers and it affects the teams' capacities to improve their work processes, customer satisfaction, and supplier performance.

The position of continuous team development in the model is intended to suggest that the primary strategy for improving the relationships that teams have with their customers and suppliers begins with including suppliers and customers as members of the team.[1] The specific characteristics of this context are outlined later in this chapter.

The information that the model communicates is as follows: we must focus on our customers and improve customer satisfaction; we must examine all our work processes and improve them or eliminate the unnecessary ones; and we must improve the performance of our suppliers. In addition, the model affirms that the capacity of teams to do any of these things depends on the context of continuous team development within which teams exist and work with their suppliers and customers. This context, like every other component in the model, must be understood and targeted for improvement.

Roles

The model includes three roles that teams occupy and among which they move. These roles are *supplier, processor,* and *customer.*

---

[1]A term that has gained in popularity to describe the ideal relationship between supplier and customer is "partnering." This term does not convey anything more specific than "team" and "teamwork"; it is yet another bit of training jargon. I use the terms team, teamwork, and team development to include all that might be conveyed by "partnering."

All these roles are present as services and products are delivered and exchanged among teams within the same organization and among teams from different organizations. The services and products in a manufacturing company are different from those in a bank or hospital, but in every exchange of input and output there are the three roles of supplier, processor, and customer.

In the center component of the model, the three roles are kept together to show that a team is always shifting among these roles. The improvement opportunities that teams identify depend on the roles they adopt at any one time. Opportunities derived from the model are:

1. As a *supplier,* the team has the goals of improving and measuring output, customers' satisfaction, and the level of team development that exists between the team and its customers;

2. As a *processor,* the team has the goals of improving and measuring work processes and improving and measuring the level of its own team development; and

3. As a *customer,* the team has the goals of improving and measuring the input from its suppliers and the level of team development that exists between the team and its suppliers.

Input and Output

The roles of suppliers, processors, and customers are connected in the model by the flows of information, materials, supplies, people, etc., that are labeled "input" and "output." As suppliers, teams focus on the satisfaction of their customers with the teams' outputs of services and products. As customers, teams focus on their own satisfaction with the input of services and products from their suppliers.

A Model for Continuous Improvement and Measurement   21

Data Links

In the model, data links are drawn between the team, the context of team development, and the team's processes, customers, and suppliers. These links have two loops. One loop is *initiating;* the other is *receiving.*

Improvement depends on the team's initiating or creating various data links between itself and the four areas of opportunity, customer satisfaction, work processes, etc. Improvement also depends on ensuring that there are links to receive and use the data requested. In the model, the team is envisioned as continually requesting and receiving data about its customers, its suppliers, its work processes, and its level of team development.

The data links are the keys to continuous improvement. They represent the flow of data that permits teams to identify how they are currently performing as well as to anticipate what they should be doing in the future. Data links serve both to give *feedback* information about what has occurred as well as to give *forward feed* information about what the team should be planning to do in the future; e.g., anticipate changes in customers' needs, anticipate how to take advantage of new technology, etc.

It is by actually creating these links that we can best appraise a team's commitment to continuous improvement. Often, the most difficult and time-consuming task in continuous improvement is to design and use data links.

The emphasis on data links in the model communicates at least one subtlety about improvement that we can easily overlook. Our improvement initiatives are going to be only as demonstrable and useful as the data links that we put in place. For example, we must not only focus on improving customer satisfaction; we must continually look for opportunities to improve the ways in which we obtain feedback from our customers. Also, we must not only improve the context that influences the performance of teams; we must also look for ways to improve how we measure this context. It is not enough to focus on improving the performance of some work process; we also must ensure that our data links with that process are regularly evaluated so that they give us the kinds of data we need to monitor the performance of the process accurately.

Data links have meaning and can be given specific content only in relation to improving something, e.g., customer satisfaction. Data links are, therefore, discussed in later chapters in connection with improving team development, output, customer satisfaction, work processes, and supplier performance.

Parallel Activities in Continuous Improvement			
Team Development	**Output and Customer Satisfaction**	**Work Processes**	**Input and Supplier Performance**
Goal: Constant improvement in capacity to function as a superior team.	**Goal:** Constant improvement in how much customers value products and services.	**Goal:** Constant improvement in every aspect of all work processes by which products and services are produced.	**Goal:** Constant improvement in quality of input and total performance of suppliers.
General Strategy: Use Model for Superior Team Development to baseline and measure team's level of development as a superior work team.	**General Strategy:** Include customers on team and use measures of customer satisfaction developed jointly with customers to continually improve output and customer satisfaction.	**General Strategy:** Measure baseline performance of all work processes and continually work on improvements.	**General Strategy:** Include suppliers on team and use measures of team's satisfaction developed jointly with suppliers to continually improve input and supplier performance.

Figure 2-2. The General Design for Continuous Improvement

Unlimited Opportunities To Improve

Opportunities for improvement are unlimited. The primary focus always is on customers and their satisfaction. In order to achieve this satisfaction, it may be appropriate, at one particular time, to emphasize work processes. At another time, it will be important to emphasize supplier performance and input. At yet another time, it may be critical to emphasize the context of team development.

Every component in the model is tied directly or indirectly to every other component by input and output or by data links. The model conveys the idea that improvements in one element will suggest improvements in another element. If we improve the context of work, people will exert more influence, become more competent, develop more commitment, and find more ways to improve the team's performance. The better we are able to satisfy our customers, the more we will raise their expectations for continuous improvement in our products and services. Once we find ways to improve one work process, we will transfer our improvements to other processes.

One additional observation about the model is that the positions of customer, processor, and supplier are interchangeable. Within organizations and among teams, movement among these three positions may take place many times per day. A fabrication shop is a supplier when it delivers its finished products to the installation mechanics. It is a customer when the engineers give it drawings and designs.

In the following sections of this chapter, I will describe the meaning of each component of the model. The order in which I discuss the components of the model does not suggest that planning and initiating improvement projects should follow this same order, although they might. Team development must begin and continue parallel with all other initiatives (Figure 2-2).

Teams must begin to measure and improve customer satisfaction to give the proper focus to all their other improvement initiatives. But some teams (e.g., those that already are functioning well as teams) might easily start with their work processes or supplier performance. So long as teams begin with a comprehensive picture of the multiple opportunities for improvement and measurement and the interrelationships of these opportunities, where they begin might as well be one place as another.

Developing the habit of continuous improvement is more important for most teams than is the kind of improvement targets they select. The one exception, of course, is that all teams must first determine whether they are functioning well enough as teams to have the potential to undertake anything other than their own development. A work group truly must function as a team if it is to undertake continuous improvement in any area other than its own improvement. The higher the levels of continuous improvement in customer satisfaction, work processes, and supplier performance, the higher the levels of team development that are required.

CONTEXT OF CONTINUOUS TEAM DEVELOPMENT

The first component in the model to be discussed is the context of continuous team development. With the rush toward identifying improvement projects related to customer satisfaction and improved work processes, it is easy to overlook the critical importance that this context has for continuous improvement. In the model, the context of team development surrounds the entire primary system of continuous improvement and is an implicit factor in every improvement project. Improvements in this context always will run parallel to every other kind of improvement. For example, a team will improve its capacity to improve its work processes to the degree to which it truly becomes a team. It will improve supplier performance to the degree to which it is able to make its suppliers part of the team.

Context defines a very specific component in continuous improvement. It defines the perceived characteristics of team development that both describe the level of team development and predict the capacity of a work group or unit to perform as a team. In an earlier work (Kinlaw, 1991), I have shown that there are four sets of characteristics that distinguish superior teams: leadership, results, informal systems, and feelings. Further information about these characteristics and the Model for Superior Team Development and Performance is found in the Appendix.

Throughout this book, the context of team development is assumed to provide the sufficient condition for continuous improvement. In the discussions that follow about the relationships between the three roles of supplier, processor, and customer, it is always assumed that these relationships are optimized as the occupants of these roles include one another as team members. When specific improvement projects are discussed in later chapters, it also is assumed that teams are sufficiently developed to initiate and manage these projects.

CUSTOMER

TQM and continuous-improvement initiatives represent an intense focus on the customer. The term *internal customer* has been created to emphasize the need for each person and team to consider all users as customers. We are even beginning to see the term "customer" applied in professions and occupations that are accustomed to using terms such as "client" and "patient."

Planning and initiating continuous improvement begins with the customer and with seeing ourselves in the role of suppliers. Two questions must be answered: (a) Who are our customers? and (b) How shall we view our customers?

Who Are Our Customers?

The term "internal customer" may not survive the current period of initiation of TQM on a large scale in this country. The relationship between suppliers, processors, and internal customers is much more complex and difficult to define than is the relationship between suppliers, processors, and *external* customers. Are managers the customers of supervisors? Are supervisors the customers of employees? When the word "customer" is used to define the relationship between a person or group lower down in an organization's hierarchy and a person or group higher up in an organization's hierarchy, there is a danger that the "higher ups" may use the term to control and exploit the "lower downs."

There also is a possibility that, by using the term "internal customer," we may dilute the meaning of "external customer" and even suggest to people that internal and external customers carry the same weight. Nevertheless, having recognized that the use of "internal customer" might be short lived and might cause some confusion, I still think that it should be used to emphasize the way in which we should think about internal organizational relationships when we consider opportunities for continuous improvement.

A customer is any person or group whom you must satisfy in order to achieve and maintain reputation, image, market share, more challenging work, profit, or the like. A customer is any person or group who influences your current and future success.

This last sentence in the definition of customer is of critical importance. It implies that my relationship with my customer is not made up of a single transaction. It implies that there always is some reason and opportunity to improve continually the quality of the services and products that I deliver to my customer.

I drive my car up and down Interstate Highway I-95 several times a year in traveling from Norfolk, Virginia, to our second office in Florida. I do not think that it is in the minds of the people who run the various gasoline stations where I might stop for gas to think of me as a valued customer anymore than I think of them as valued suppliers. Our relationship is momentary and is defined largely by chance. The operators of these stations are not looking for me to stop again, and I don't expect to do so. My requests are kept to a minimum, and their service is kept to a minimum. There is little reason for these operators to consider constantly improving their service for a customer they may never see again.

The exception to the foregoing description is when service stations are part of a chain, like fast-food restaurants, and repeat business among the various franchises of the chain establishes the condition of long-term relationship.

One key step in continuous improvement is to identify all our customers and to become quite clear about their impact on us. Being quite clear about who our external customers are can be an important factor in organizational survival or demise.

Some months ago, I was asked to help a group that provided employee-assistance programs for a number of companies on the East Coast. Early in the process, I helped the group to identify its external customers. At the start, the group identified the employees that used its counseling and training services as its primary customers. As our discussion progressed, it became obvious that the group's key customers were not just the people who were direct users of their services. They also were the managers and senior executives who made decisions about the group's contracts.

Continuous improvement of customer satisfaction can take place only when we have accurately defined who our customers are. In addition, improvement in market share can be created by recognizing who might become our external customers.

Peter Drucker (1974) describes the remarkable advantages that the carpet industry achieved when it ceased to define its primary customers as homeowners and began to define its primary customers as mass builders and developers. The industry recognized that it could capture its new customers by showing builders how they could build cheaper and better homes by using wall-to-wall carpeting to cover cheap flooring.

Zenger/Miller, a large producer of off-the-shelf training programs, is another example of a company that has greatly increased its market share by recognizing that it has more than one customer. When the company began, it considered its primary customers to be members of the training staffs in organizations. Now its primary customers are the executives and managers who decide how the companies' budgets will be spent on training.

How Shall We View Our Customers?

Organizational literature usually has defined quality to mean meeting a preset standard or specification. TQM, however, defines quality as whatever the customer says is quality. One key message in TQM is that quality exists when the customer says it exists. The customer is the final arbiter of quality. Quality includes the measured characteristics or performance of a service or product and a lot more. It includes a variety of "soft" variables, such as taste, fashion, trends, attractiveness, feel, courtesy, responsiveness, friendliness, proactiveness, and a host of other intangibles that influence customer satisfaction.

Improving customer satisfaction requires a great deal more than improving the measurable standards of a product or service. It also requires exceeding the customer's expectations and accepting the customer's perceptions as real data.

AT&T has recognized that the explosion of information and the expansion of global markets has greatly increased the expectations of its customers regarding quality of service. It operates on the assumption that a market leader must be rated "excellent" by its customers if it is to retain 90 percent of its market share. AT&T's service strategy is to evaluate customer expectations in three tiers (Schulman & Salvolaine, 1990):

- establishment of the connection,
- quality of the connection, and
- value of the connection.

Each tier builds on the preceding and creates an integrated process for assessing the perceptions and expectations of international customers. The goal of this assessment process is to identify and evaluate all the critical variables in international telecommunications that determine customer satisfaction.

The roles of internal customers and external customers differ most in the degree of power that they can exert over a team's success or future. Improving the satisfaction of external customers is an *involuntary* requirement. To stay in business or to enlarge our market share, we *must* continuously improve the satisfaction of the people and companies who pay for our services and products—our external customers.

One subtlety that may be involved in the early stages of initiating continuous improvement is that teams must *voluntarily* give their internal customers power that these customers might not heretofore have had. Teams can do this in several steps.

1. First, they can identify all the people and groups who are users of their services and products and begin to refer to them as customers.

2. Next, teams can develop ways to measure the satisfaction of their internal customers.

3. Third, they can publish their measurement of the satisfaction of their internal customers and make that information available to everyone in the total organization.

As TQM develops and matures in an organization, the requirement to improve the satisfaction of internal customers can be institutionalized by requiring every team to identify its customers, measure their satisfaction, and publicize these measurements. In addition, organizations can develop a variety of special awards to acknowledge the achievements of teams in satisfying their internal customers.

In Chapter 5, I will describe in detail various tools for improving and measuring customer satisfaction.

The General Strategy for Improving Customer Satisfaction

Team development is the grand strategy for the three critical events that underlie continuous improvement. It is through team development that teams:

1. Equip themselves for continuous improvement;

2. Include customers as part of their teams, improve their output, and assure that the satisfaction of their customers is continuously improved; and

3. Include suppliers as part of their teams, improve the input of their suppliers, and assure that the performance of their suppliers is continuously improved.

Team development is the *context* within which continuous improvement is initiated and maintained between the three roles of supplier, processor, and customer.

The meaning of *team,* as applied to external customers, may differ from the meaning of team when applied to internal customers. This difference will be one of degree only. The critical dimensions of team development are the same, e.g., inclusion, commitment, loyalty, pride, and trust (Kinlaw, 1991).

OUTPUT

This presentation of an overview of the Model for Continuous Improvement and Measurement (Figure 2-1), first assumes the perspective of the role of *supplier.* As suppliers, we must focus first on our customers and on customer satisfaction.

The supply link between supplier and customer is the output of services and products that the supplier delivers to the customer. In this section, I will provide a general description of output along with an overview of how output fits into the general design for continuous improvement.

Output, in the Model for Continuous Improvement and Measurement, refers to any service or product that is delivered through one or more processes. Output, therefore, has two components: (a) the *service or product* produced; and (b) the *delivery* of the service or product to the customer. The first component, service or product, cannot be improved directly; it can only be measured. The second component, delivery, is a process and it, like all processes, can be improved directly.

Because delivery is a process, it is best to include it with all other work processes in planning and initiating improvement. Unless I state otherwise, therefore, output will refer to services and products.

Output cannot be considered by itself in improving and measuring continuous improvement. The *reason* that we improve output is to improve customer satisfaction. The *way* that we improve output is by improving the processes that produce the output. As we think about identifying opportunities for improvement, we must consider output in connection with customer satisfaction and in connection with the processes that produce the output.

Measuring output can answer questions such as:

- What is the output costing?
- How long does it take to produce it?
- Is the output within our standards?
- What kinds of errors are occurring?
- What is the frequency of the errors?

Where and how we measure output depends on the process in which we are interested. In the preparation of a travel authorization, we might consider the flow as starting with a request for travel authorization (input) and going on to reimbursement for travel (output). But we might choose to study a smaller process, from the request for travel (input) to the act of obtaining approval (output).

Measuring output largely is a matter of formulating useful ratios so that the output is compared to something else, e.g., revision of computer software compared to hours of labor, completed repair orders compared to time, number of parts produced compared to the number falling outside quality standards, etc. In Chapter 5, I will describe a number of these ratios and the process for writing them.

PROCESSOR

In the foregoing discussion, we have looked at improvement and measurement from the perspective of a supplier to its customers. In this section, I will take the perspective of a *processor* and give an overview of the continuous improvement and measurement opportunities that are represented by the multitude of processes by which work is accomplished. When one is in the role of supplier, one also is in the role of processor. It is as processors that we are able to be suppliers.

Statistical process control, systems improvement, total quality systems, and continuous systems improvement are some of the phrases current in TQM that underscore the emphasis on work processes. One of the popular statements in TQM is: "If you continue to do it the same way, you will continue to get the same results."

A characteristic of any team is that it is a processor and uses repeatable or repetitive steps and sequences to produce its products or services. People in a facilities-maintenance group receive a trouble report and go through a routine to process the report, make the repair, and close out the report. Software-support teams receive requests for new or upgraded software, put together a project group, and proceed through a sequence of activities to produce the software.

Throughout this book, I use the terms process, flow, step, and operation with the following meanings. A *process* is the *flow* of some object through a sequence of *steps* that include *transport, delay, operations, and inspection.* An object is whatever is moved or changed. An object may be a report, idea, metal stock, or car frame. All individuals and teams perform some step or operation in a variety of processes.

The only steps that are truly productive in any process are operations. Our goal in continuous process improvement should be to reduce or eliminate every other step, while eliminating all errors associated with every step. Operations are the only steps that cannot all be eliminated.

Figure 2-3 may help you to visualize the relationship between a process and an operation. The process is shown flowing in a horizontal direction through various steps. Operations are shown as vertical intersections of the step-to-step flow in a process in which some action is taken to transform the object or idea flowing through the process.

Operations can occur through human or automated action. Spot welds on a car frame can be done by people or by robots. Signatures on checks can be written by people or by signature machines.

Improving a process presents an enormous opportunity for continuous improvement for at least four reasons:

1. Processes are present everywhere, and the large number of them presents to teams an enormous area of opportunity;

2. Any improvement in a process will have a positive effect on the output of the process and, consequently, on customer satisfaction;

3. Improvements in processes will have much larger and more lasting effects than the improvement of any one worker's performance; and

4. Opportunities to improve any one process are endless.

Various tools for improving work processes are described in Chapter 6.

INPUT AND SUPPLIER

In the foregoing description of the Model for Continuous Improvement and Measurement, I have discussed continuous improvement and measurement from the perspectives of supplier and processor. In this section, I will discuss *input and supplier* from the perspective of customer.

Simplified Manufacturing Process

INPUT ... **OUTPUT**

STEP	Delay	Transport	Operation →	Transport	Delay	Operation →	Transport	etc.
DESCRIPTION	Storage	Move Raw Materials to Machine	Cut	Move to Next Machine	Wait in Line	De-burr	Move to Storage	

PROCESS ——————————————————————————————————▶

Simplified Engineering Process

INPUT ... **OUTPUT**

STEP	Operation →	Transport	Operation →	Transport	Delay	Inspect	Transport	etc.
DESCRIPTION	Drawing Request	Deliver Request to Drafter	Prepare Drawing	Deliver Drawing to Engineer	Drawing Waiting for Engineer	Verify Drawing	Deliver to Printing	

PROCESS ——————————————————————————————————▶

Figure 2-3. Relationship of Operations to Process

Much of the descriptions of output and customer satisfaction can, with slight modification, be transferred to the discussion of input and supplier. Just as there are internal and external customers, there are internal and external suppliers. The same sort of complexity that I described in a team's relationship as supplier to its internal customers pertains in a team's relationship as customer to its internal suppliers. Just as our customers are the final arbiters of the value of the services and products that we deliver to them, so are we the final arbiters of the value of the services and products delivered to us. Just as it is to our advantage to include our customers on our team, it is also to our advantage to avoid adversarial and arms-length relationships with our suppliers and to include them on our team.

Just as the term "internal customer" may not survive the current period of initiating TQM on a large scale in this country, so may the use of the term "internal supplier" be short lived. At the time this book is being written, however, internal customer and internal supplier have common acceptance in most organizations and they do serve the useful purpose of emphasizing how we should think about internal organizational relationships (mutual interdependence) when we consider opportunities for continuous improvement.

All persons and all teams have suppliers who deliver various kinds of inputs to them, which they process and turn into their own outputs of services and products. A supplier is any person or group who should satisfy us and help us to achieve, maintain, or improve reputation, image, market share, more challenging work, profit, etc.

This last sentence in the definition of supplier is of critical importance. It implies that our relationship with our suppliers is not made up of a single transaction. It implies that there is some reason and opportunity to improve constantly the quality of the services and products that we receive from suppliers.

Suppliers are individuals and groups to whom our own improvement and success are tied. Improvements in a team's work processes, output, and customer satisfaction depend on the performance of its suppliers and the services and products (input) that they deliver.

The practical steps that teams need to take to improve the services and products that they receive from their internal and external suppliers are:

1. Identify all the people and groups who are suppliers of services and products to the team;
2. Develop mutually agreeable ways to measure the team's satisfaction with the services and products that it receives;
3. Make public and generally available the measurements of the team's satisfaction with its suppliers; and
4. Develop ways to use the data on supplier performance to improve that performance.

This four-step approach is designed to establish a collaborative relationship with suppliers and to make them part of the team's process of continuous improvement. The idea of making the supplier part of the customer's team is contrary to the adversarial relationship that has often marked customers' relationships with their external suppliers and which has been part of customers' relationships with their internal suppliers.

Traditional Customer and Supplier Relationships

One of the major problems that customers have in improving the performance of their suppliers (especially the external ones) is that they often develop an adversarial relationship or a relationship based on power. Both customer and supplier suffer as a result of such relationships.

One of my friends taught project management in a large aerospace engineering firm for many years. In discussing the relationships of project managers to their contractors he often would say:

Some of you have learned not to trust your contractors and have been taught that you must "hold the contractor's feet to the fire." I promise you that, if you follow that philosophy, the only thing you will get are burned feet.

If we approach our relationships with our external suppliers as being based on power, we develop these relationships based on what we see as the current balance of power between ourselves and our customers (Buffa, 1984). To ensure that the balance of power is in our favor as customers, we then try to ensure that we:

- Keep criteria for supplier performance vague or unavailable;
- Standardize our requirements so that they can be met by multiple suppliers;
- Purchase a significant fraction of our supplier's output;
- Keep suppliers vulnerable by ensuring that their margin of profit is low on what we use; and
- Maintain a credible threat that we might become our own suppliers.

We pay an enormous price by developing arm's-length relationships with our suppliers—ones that are based on distrust, power, and threat. This price is apparent in our government's relationship with its suppliers, most of whom are contractors. The litany of contract overruns and the recurring purchase of simple items such as hammers and washers at hundreds of times their market value attests vividly to this price.

The just-in-time (JIT) method of supply developed by Toyota in Japan is an excellent example of a collaborative and mutually interdependent relationship between customer and supplier. The goal of JIT is the total elimination of waste. As applied to inventory, this means the complete elimination of inventory. JIT means to produce what is needed, when it is needed, with what is needed.

JIT is made possible only by the development of long-term, stable relationships between customers and suppliers. Sufficient trust must be developed so that suppliers will build plants near their customers in order to reduce transportation time.

Edinburgh Napier University

Customer name: **XIAOFEI, LIU**

Title: Continuous improvement and
measurement for total quality :
D: 38042001860376
Due: 24 March 2011

Total items: 1
24/02/2011 18:26
Checked out: 6

Any comments? Let us know at
ibraryfeedback@napier.ac.uk

JIT purchase agreements tend to emphasize product performance and to avoid over-specification of other requirements. Agreements avoid stipulating how a product must be produced and leave suppliers with ample room to innovate.

One major opportunity to improve the performance of external suppliers is to change the relationship of customer and supplier into one that is characterized by teamwork and team development. When we analyze the dimensions of these desired relationships, they look very much like many of the dimensions that are associated with superior work teams (Kinlaw, 1991).

The General Strategy for Improving Input and Supplier Performance

The general strategy for continuous improvement is to strengthen the context of continuous team development. Team development is the *context* within which continuous improvement is initiated and maintained between the three roles of supplier, processor, and customer. It follows that the general strategy for improving input and supplier performance is to make suppliers feel and act like members of the customer's team. The meaning of team as applied to external suppliers may differ in degree from its meaning when applied to internal suppliers. But the difference will be one of degree only. The critical dimensions of team development are the same, i.e., inclusion, commitment, loyalty, pride, and trust.

SUMMARY OF GENERAL STRATEGY FOR CONTINUOUS IMPROVEMENT

From the foregoing description of the Model for Continuous Improvement and Measurement and the discussion of each of the components of the model, there emerges a General Design for Continuous Improvement (Figure 2-2). The design is derived from the Model for Continuous Improvement and Measurement and shows that continuous improvement results from four parallel initiatives, each of which is characterized by a general strategy.

Continuous improvement must touch every aspect of a team's life and work. The goals of the four initiatives must be addressed continually and pursued arduously, and the general strategies of the four initiatives must underlie all specific improvement projects. A team must give continual attention to:

1. The continuous improvement of its own level of development as a superior team;

2. The inclusion of its customers on the team, the continuous improvement of the measured quality of the team's output, and the measured satisfaction of its customers;

3. The continuous improvement of all the team's work processes; and

4. The inclusion of the suppliers on the team and the continuous improvement of the measured quality of its suppliers' input and performance.

In this chapter, the Model for Continuous Improvement and Measurement is described, and a brief overview is presented of the information communicated by the model and how teams might use it as they plan for continuous improvement. The next chapter will provide a process for designing improvement projects. In the following chapters, we will be concerned with the specific tools that can be used in teams' improvement projects as they focus on the contexts of team development, customer satisfaction, work processes, and supplier performance.

Chapter 3

*A General Design for
Improvement and
Measurement Projects*

Continuous improvement results from specific improvement projects. It is the synergetic effect of all the specific improvement projects undertaken by every formal and informal team in an organization.

Continuous improvement does not result from a single initiative or special emphasis. It does not result from programs, policies, special promotions, and banners. It does not result directly from vague schemes to change managers' styles or improve job satisfaction or from strategies to overhaul an organization's culture.

Continuous improvement results from the persistent, concrete, day-to-day search to make every aspect of performance better. *Improvement becomes continuous when it no longer is viewed as special—when it is viewed as work.*

Organizations and teams do, of course, require a vision. People must have some reasonable clarity about "the grand scheme of things." But visions and goals must be translated into work. Projects are the way in which executive pronouncements and organizational-improvement goals are translated into results.

Improvement projects may be large or small. They may be as simple as increasing the availability of a supervisor to team members or reducing the number of non-value-added signatures in the preparation of a report. They may be as complex as combining two or more automated information systems or reducing the steps in the preparation of a corporate budget. Whatever the level of complexity, improvement projects must be given a shape. They must be designed.

The purpose of this chapter is to provide the outline of a design that can be applied to all improvement projects. In subsequent chapters, this design will be applied to the four kinds of improvement targets: team development, customer satisfaction, work processes, and supplier performance.

GENERAL CHARACTERISTICS OF IMPROVEMENT PROJECTS

Improvement projects conform to the following general characteristics. They are:

- team-centered and team-driven,
- structured and systematic,
- biased toward proactivity,
- based on data and measurable, and
- long-term in emphasis.

Team-Centered and Team-Driven

Improvement projects are team projects. If they are to be successful, they require the cooperation and collaboration of a number of people from start to finish. They are designed and implemented by a work team, a management team, a customer-supplier team, a special team, or one of the many other kinds of teams that exist as part of a normal organization or that have been created for a particular purpose.

Structured and Systematic

Improvement projects should systematically follow a predetermined flow or set of steps, should conform to certain, predetermined criteria (e.g., being measurable), and should be monitored and managed by an established process. Improvement projects should have the general characteristics of any other successful projects. These projects require a plan that ensures that they meet their objectives and stay on schedule. Later in this chapter are six principal steps for designing improvement projects.

Biased Toward Proactivity

I have emphasized at several points in this book that continuous improvement means a great deal more than "putting out fires," correcting mistakes, controlling damage, or repairing what is failing or getting ready to fail. Such improvements primarily are *repairs* (Figure 1-1).

The design for improvement projects presented in this chapter certainly can be used to troubleshoot problems. However, in order to make improvement constant, we must take what is already working and make it better. We must spend more time *preventing* problems in quality than we do in correcting problems in quality. The general design for improvement projects described in this chapter helps a team to find opportunities to make even better what is already working satisfactorily.

Based on Data and Measurable

All improvement projects are measurement projects. Improvement projects are not based on bias or whim; they are based on data. Improvement projects define opportunities and problems with numbers, and their performance is tracked with numbers.

Improvement projects are based on questions such as "How many?" "How often?" "How long?" and "To what degree?" They start with questions such as "How long does the process take?" "How many pits were there in the part?" "What is the cost to produce the report?" and "How much time is spent correcting design errors?"

Long-Term in Emphasis

Improvement projects should focus on underlying causes and on changes that can make a substantive and long-term impact on performance. The major emphasis in TQM initiatives, quite naturally, has been on improving work processes. Improving work processes is the most obvious way to prevent both the occurrence and recurrence of problems. Improving work processes is the only way to achieve substantive and long-term effects in the quality of services and products.

Long-term improvement is a consequence of continuous improvement. Long-term results can be achieved only when continuous and systematic attention is given to improving every aspect of work. The Model for Continuous Improvement and Measurement encourages systematic improvement that will produce long-term results.

TQM TOOLS

Before describing each of the key steps in the design of improvement projects, I will present some of the TQM tools that are integral to such design. I will refer to these tools and give examples of their use later, as I discuss the various steps for designing improvement projects. Without an understanding of these tools, teams will have great difficulty in designing improvement projects that are substantial and satisfying.

Most TQM tools can be used at more than one of the steps in the design of improvement projects. Figure 3-1 outlines the tools that are mentioned in this book and relates them to the steps for designing improvement projects.

Additional information about a number of TQM tools is provided in the Appendix. This is so the reader need spend time obtaining detailed information only about some of the more important tools that he or she is not already able to use. As is mentioned in the Introduction, however, I have not provided detailed information about TQM tools and statistics that is already available in many other publications (e.g., Ishikawa, 1985; Montgomery, 1985; Ott, 1975; Wheeler & Chambers, 1986).

Improvement Project Steps	TQM Tools
1. Understand the Opportunity or Problem	*Models *Brainstorming *Nominal Group Technique *Surveys *Flow Charts *Cause-and-Effect Diagrams *Pareto Charts *Histograms *Run Charts *Scatter Diagrams *Control Charts
2. Define the Specific Improvement Target	*Flow Charts *Cause-and-Effect Diagrams *Pareto Charts *Histograms *Scatter Diagrams
3. Design Strategies To Reach the Target	*Models *Brainstorming *Nominal Group Technique *Cause-and-Effect Diagrams
4. Design the Data Links	*Surveys *Observations *Devices (mechanical, electronic, pneumatic, optical) *Interviews
5. Design the Response Process To Use Data from the Data Links	*Pareto Charts *Histograms *Control Charts
6. Determine How the Project Will Be Managed	*Project Management Sheets *Milestone Charts

Figure 3-1. Project Steps and TQM Tools

TQM tools can be divided conveniently into the following categories:

- **Models**. These are graphics (pictures or diagrams) that assist teams in understanding and planning improvement. The Model for Continuous Improvement and Measurement (Figure 2-1) is an example. The model that shows the relationship of operations to a process (Figure 2-3) is another.

- **Rational/Structured**. These are tools that provide an orderly process for accomplishing tasks such as developing information, identifying likely causes, creating alternatives, and making decisions. Examples are the brainstorming process, flow charts, interviews, and cause-and-effect diagrams.

- **Numerical/Statistical**. These are tools that can be used to count, to show mathematical relationships, and to measure the performance of work processes. Examples are run charts, Pareto charts, histograms, surveys that produce data that can be manipulated statistically, and control charts.

MODELS

There are many models that can assist teams in designing improvement projects. In two earlier works (Kinlaw, 1989; 1991), I describe a number of such models. In this section, however, I will include only two models. The first, the Model for Continuous Improvement and Measurement, provides the framework within which improvement projects are designed. The second, the Model for Superior Team Development and Performance, is discussed briefly in Chapter 2. It defines team development and provides the guidance that teams need to pursue this major opportunity for improvement.

The Model for Continuous Improvement and Measurement

This book is based on the notion that the primary tool for continuous improvement is the Model for Continuous Improvement and Measurement. This model is a tool. It provides teams with a conceptual overview of continuous improvement and identifies for them the four major areas of opportunity:

- team development,
- output and customer satisfaction,
- work processes, and
- input and supplier performance.

The model should be introduced to teams early, as they begin to identify improvement opportunities and start to translate these opportunities into specific projects.

The Model for Superior Team Development and Performance

Team development is a prior condition for continuous improvement. It must be addressed as directly and as specifically as all other opportunities for improvement. Teams can use the Model for Superior Team Development and Performance (see Chapter 2 and the Appendix) to understand what superior teams are like, to identify their own opportunities for growth, and to track their progress. The model can be used as a discussion tool, and surveys based on the model can be used to develop numerical baselines.

Uses of Models

Models are particularly useful to help teams to:
- conceptualize the steps and elements in a process or action;
- think systemically and understand the interrelationships between variables and elements involved in an improvement project;
- plan an action or project; and
- create new and better models from old ones.

RATIONAL/STRUCTURED TOOLS

There are an extraordinarily large number of structured tools that can be used to develop information and make decisions (van

Grundy, 1985). There also are many tools to be used in creating alternatives and identifying causes and antecedents for problems and opportunities. The descriptions below are of those tools that have demonstrated general utility. Additional information about the tools covered in this section is found in the Appendix.

Brainstorming

This is by far the most widely used (and abused) tool for developing information. It was originated around 1938 by Alex Osborn (1979). Brainstorming follows a structured sequence of steps that is based on two general principles: (a) deferred judgment and (b) the quality of ideas as a function of the quantity of ideas. The basic rules followed in brainstorming are: (a) ideas may not be criticized; (b) free association of ideas is encouraged; (c) the more ideas that can be created the better; and (d) ideas should stimulate other ideas.

Nominal Group Technique

The nominal group technique (NGT) is similar to brainstorming but is more structured. Ideas are generated in writing and are not identified with the individuals who generate them. NGT also employs a weighted decision-making process.

This tool can be a great help to teams that are not yet fully formed and in which members have concerns about rank and position. It encourages the open discussion of ideas and helps the team to avoid unnecessary conflict between members.

Flow Charts

A flow chart is a graphic representation of a work process, with all the steps and operations in the process identified. This helps people to understand the work process. Flow charts can tell us how something is done, when it gets done, and where specific steps occur.

Figure 3-2 (page 50) is a simple example of a flow chart that shows the steps and operations in the process for cashing a check in a bank.

Cause-and-Effect Diagrams

Cause-and-effect diagrams also are known as fishbone, Ishikawa, or "why?" diagrams. These diagrams can be used to identify the possible causes of a problem or to identify actions that might be taken to reach an improvement target. These diagrams are a way of visually displaying an effect and then: (a) identifying the causes (or factors) that account for the effect; (b) grouping these causes into categories or classes; and (c) selecting the cause or group of causes that might be removed (in the case of a problem) or created (in the case of an improvement initiative).

Figure 3-3 (page 51) is an example of a cause-and-effect diagram that identifies possible causes associated with poor gas mileage.

Uses of Rational/Structured Tools

These tools can help teams to do the following:

- become more efficient and effective in their team sessions,
- create ideas and information,
- understand processes,
- make orderly and consensual decisions,
- identify causes related to problems, and
- generate strategies for action.

NUMERICAL/STATISTICAL TOOLS

The final group of TQM tools are the ones that use numbers and statistics. These tools not only help teams to understand their

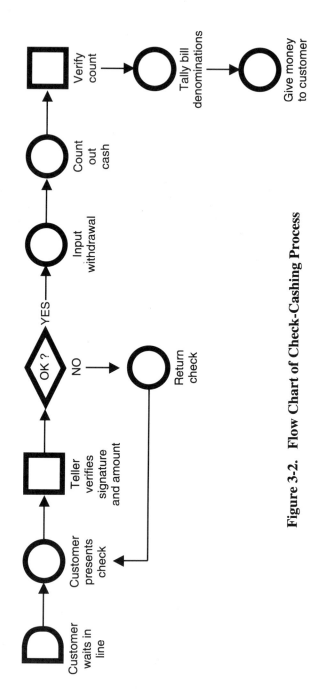

Figure 3-2. Flow Chart of Check-Cashing Process

Continuous Improvement and Measurement for Total Quality

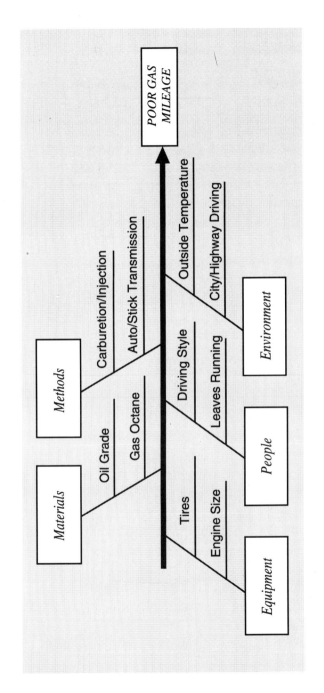

Figure 3-3. Cause-and-Effect Diagram for Poor Mileage

problems and opportunities but they also help teams to become quite specific about their improvement targets.

Surveys

Not all surveys produce numbers or results that can be manipulated statistically. However, the kind of surveys that are the most useful in developing information for improving teams and their performance are designed to produce numbers that can be reduced, analyzed, and used to make decisions. Surveys can be used to collect data about perceptions and opinions. They can be effectively used to determine such things as:

- levels of team development,
- quality of team meetings,
- degrees of customer satisfaction,
- quality of work environments,
- performance of supervisors and managers,
- satisfaction with input and supplier performance, and
- perceptions of interface problems among teams and organizations.

Surveys can be simple or complex. They can be designed to retrieve information about many variables or just a few. Whether they are simple or complex, they can be quite difficult to construct.

Figure 3-4 is an example of a survey form that could be used to measure participant satisfaction in a training program. It shows how much information can be obtained with very few questions. This survey tells us how satisfied the customer was, what needs to be changed, and what the prospects are in the marketplace for such programs.

Surveys are discussed further in Chapters 4 and 5; additional examples of surveys are included in the Appendix.

Please answer the following questions and return this survey to your instructor at the end of the program you are attending. **This is an anonymous survey. Please do NOT put your name on this sheet.**

1. What is the name of the program you have just attended?

_____

2. On what dates did you attend the program?

_____

3. What is the name of your company or organization?

_____

4. Did anything cause you any discomfort or dissatisfaction during the program? If so please describe.

5. Please check one of the following alternatives.

    a. ____ I would recommend this program, without reservation, to others.

    b. ____ I would recommend this program to others with some reservation.

    c. ____ I would not recommend this program to others.

Figure 3-4. Survey Form for Measuring Participant Satisfaction

Check Sheets

A check sheet is tally of multiple observations of a quality indicator. Check sheets commonly are used to tally things such as defective items, process-distribution checks, locations of defects, and causes for defects. Check sheets are arranged so that they automatically order data as the data are collected, provide summaries of the data, and permit easy interpretation of the data. Figure 3-5 is an example of a check sheet for errors in a procurement process.

Target: Procurement Documents	Period: Each week for 8 weeks, beginning 5/92								
	Period								
	1	2	3	4	5	6	7	8	Total
Order Nos.	8	5	3	2	2	2	3	5	30
Request Errors	3	2		4	2	1	1	1	14
Description	3	2	2	2	3	2	1	1	16
Address	2	1	2	3		1	1	1	11
Priority No.		1		2	1	2		1	7
Data Missing	4	3	2	3	3	1	1		17
Misspellings		2	1	3	2	1	1		10
Suspense Dates	1	1	1	3	1	1	1		9
All Others	1		1	1			1	1	5
Total	22	17	12	23	14	11	10	10	119

Figure 3-5. Data Sheet for Procurement Errors

Pareto Charts

A Pareto chart is a bar chart in which the bars are arranged in a descending order of size (i.e., number of observations included in the bar or class). The percentage contribution that each bar makes to the total is computed in an ascending order. The Pareto chart is useful in identifying those major causes or events that contribute most to a result or problem. The Pareto chart can help teams to decide things such as which causes of a problem are most frequent, which improvement strategies will be the most costly, or which factors contribute most to a customer's satisfaction or dissatisfaction.

An example of a Pareto chart is shown in Figure 3-6. It is based on the data used for the check sheet in Figure 3-5. The chart suggests that over 25 percent of all errors are the result of mistakes in entering the order numbers for parts and materials. By reducing this error, the team can make a rapid and significant improvement in the quality of its work.

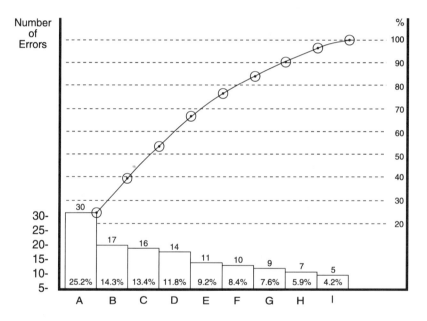

A=Order number error; B=Data missing; C=Description error; D=Request error; E=Address error; F=Misspelling; G=Wrong suspense Dates; H=Wrong priority number; I=All other sources of error

Figure 3-6. Pareto Chart of Errors in Procurement Process

Histograms

Histograms are bar charts that group the data from some distribution into classes (i.e., bars). Histograms provide a static picture of how a process is performing.

Figure 3-7 shows three examples of histogram shapes. Histogram A is symmetrical; most observations are in the middle classes. It appears that the system is behaving normally and that most variation is caused by chance.

Figure 3-7.   Sample Histogram Shapes

In histogram B, most of the measurements are bunched off to the right or skewed in that direction. The data in histogram C are concentrated at the left and right extremes (bi-modal). When looking at such distributions, a team would be prompted to ask "Why?" Possible causes of these shapes might be inaccurate data, data obtained under quite different conditions (e.g., early and late in the day), input to the system from different suppliers, etc.

An example of a histogram showing readings in ohms for a set of coils is shown in Figure 3-8. The distribution appears to be almost normal. Without additional information, we can conclude that the measured variation is attributable primarily to the cumulative effect of chance.

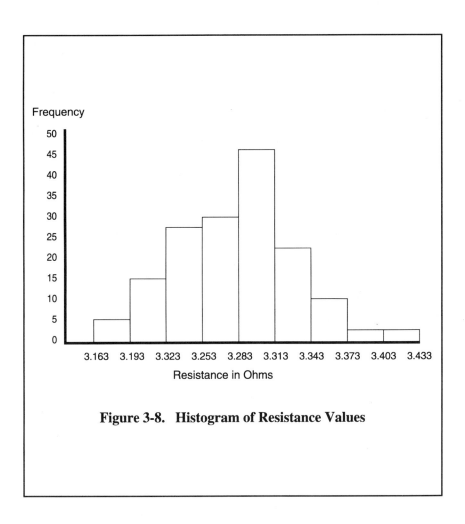

Figure 3-8. Histogram of Resistance Values

Run Charts

A run chart is a graph of one aspect of the performance of a process over a specific period of time. Run charts can be made to track things such as the number of damaged parts per shipment occurring over time, the number of errors made per report over time, the number of days it takes to complete a travel order over a period of time, and so on. An example of a run chart is found in Figure 3-9.

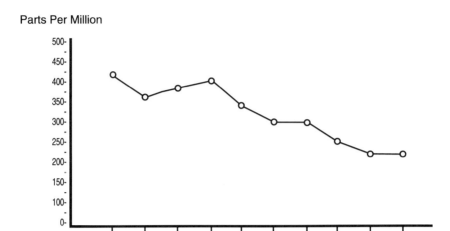

Parts Per Million

Week

Figure 3-9. Run Chart of Particulate Counts in NASA Clean Room

Control Charts

A control chart is a plot of a statistic (usually obtained from randomly selected subgroups) that shows how a work process is behaving in comparison with its statistical control limits.

The great value of control charts is that they:

1. Permit us to determine when a process is performing the best that can be expected, i.e., is under statistical control;

2. Keep us from treating general causes (those caused by chance or natural variation) as though they were special; and

3. Keep us from treating special causes (those caused by some correctable error) as though they were general.

Control charts are more complex than the TQM tools described thus far. A full description of control charts and their use is a subject unto itself, and a number of excellent references are available (Burr, 1976; Montgomery, 1985; Ott, 1975; Wheeler & Chambers, 1986). Enough information about control charts is found in this book to enable teams to begin using them. Different kinds of control charts are described in the Appendix. In the discussion of improving work processes in Chapter 6, I discuss how to develop control charts and give examples of their use. For the time being, here is one example.

Suppose a special team is put together to look at errors on weekly time cards and to reduce those errors. The team sets out first to determine what the time-card process is capable of doing. It takes a sample of time cards from each Friday's batch for ten weeks and averages the total number of errors for each batch. Suppose the average number of errors (using rounded numbers for purposes of illustration) were:

	Sample									
	1	2	3	4	5	6	7	8	9	10
Avg.	18	7	5	2	10	6	17	6	4	5

The team uses the sample error averages to make the c chart shown in Figure 3-10 (page 60). A c chart is a chart that is used when we are interested in the total number of defects, e.g., the total number of pits in the paint job of a car, the total number of typing errors in a standard report, etc.

Let's say the team finds the average errors in each sample, that is, "c," to be 8.0. It computes the upper control limit to be 16.4 and the lower control limit to be less than zero (and, therefore, irrelevant).

From the control chart, the team properly would suspect that the time-card process is behaving in a random manner and not under statistical control. Two points are outside the upper control limits. The team would need to address these errors and bring the process under control before it could make substantial improvement in the process.

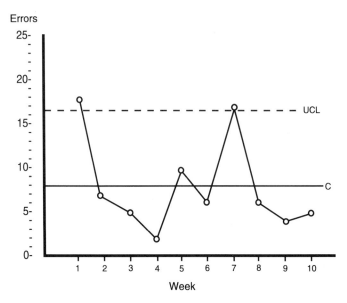

**Figure 3-10. C Chart Showing Errors in Daily Sample of Ten Cards
(Process Not Under Statistical Control)**

To continue the illustration, let us say that the team discovers that the two points on its control chart that are outside the control limits are caused in a section of the company that is experimenting with self-managed teams. After taking steps to help those self-managed teams to deliver properly prepared time cards, the team once again measures the error rate in time cards. Figure 3-11 shows the results.

In Figure 3-11, the time-card system is under statistical control, and the error rates fall within the upper and lower control limits. To reduce the error rate, the team would have to improve the total performance of the system, that is, reduce c—the average of the samples.

Scatter Diagrams

A scatter diagram is a graph that compares two characteristics of the same sample. One axis of the graph is used for one of the characteristics, and the other axis is used for the second charac-

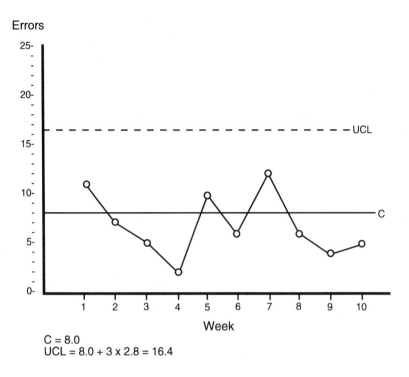

Errors

C = 8.0
UCL = 8.0 + 3 x 2.8 = 16.4

**Figure 3-11. C Chart Showing Errors in Daily Sample of Ten Time Cards
(Process Under Statistical Control)**

teristic. A scatter diagram shows how the changes in two characteristics vary together. The correlation is positive if both characteristics change together in the same direction. The correlation is
negative if the characteristics change in opposite directions on the
scatter diagram. No correlation exists when we observe no relationship in the way one characteristic changes as the other one
changes.

Scatter diagrams are useful in answering questions such as: "Is
there any relationship between the time of day and the number of
errors a team makes?" "Is there any relationship between the
supplier and the number of errors in a final product?" "Is there any
relationship between the kind of software used and the time it takes

to produce a drawing?" Figure 3-12 is a scatter diagram of the number of mistakes in time cards and the time of day on Friday that they are submitted. The diagram shows that the number of errors increases as the time of submission becomes later. This is a positive relationship. One measured characteristic is changing in the same direction as the other characteristic. However, this correlation does not mean that lateness in the day causes more mistakes.

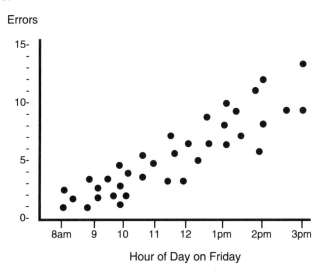

**Figure 3-12. Scatter Diagram of Time-Card Errors Compared with
Time Submitted on Friday**

Uses of Numerical/Statistical Tools

Numerical/statistical tools provide the means for acquiring and presenting data in a concrete format that permits interpretation. These tools increase our specific understanding.

Data that are collected, analyzed, and displayed by the use of data sheets, charts, and diagrams help us to judge consistency, make comparisons, and track performance. The different kinds of control charts also help us to determine how processes are working and what improvement initiatives are appropriate.

KEY STEPS IN THE DESIGN OF IMPROVEMENT PROJECTS

There are six principal steps in the design of improvement projects:

1. Understand the opportunity or problem;
2. Define the specific improvement target;
3. Design strategies to reach the target;
4. Design the data links to track performance and to anticipate necessary adjustments;
5. Design the response process to use data from the data links; and
6. Determine how the project will be managed.

The specific methods and tools that are used with each of these steps will vary with the kind of improvement opportunity that is explored and the kind of improvement target that is selected. If, for example, a team focuses on team development, it may choose to use a survey to measure the perceptions of members about a set of superior team characteristics such as inclusion, commitment, loyalty, pride, and trust. If a team focuses on its output, it will want to collect data about things such as costs and errors. If it focuses on a process, the team will need to produce a flow chart of the process, measure the time for each step in the process, measure the variation in the process, and so on.

The six steps in the design of improvement projects are interrelated and should be planned together. For example, the team will need to decide how it will measure and track an improvement in order to define the term "improvement." It also must plan how it will use the data from the data links as it selects the improvement target and designs the data links.

Step 1: Understand the Opportunity or Problem

Opportunities and problems occur in a team's work in two general ways: (a) they are forced on or assigned to the team or (b) they are discovered by the team. Customer complaints, delays in a work process, and failure to meet standards are some of the many causes that *force* teams to undertake improvement projects. Teams also may be *assigned* improvement projects by upper management or by another group (such as a quality board or continuous-improvement council) with the necessary authority. Teams may be formed to improve work processes that reach across the total organization, such as procurement processes, employee-information systems, performance-appraisal systems, training systems, and production sequences.

Improvement opportunities may occur at any of five different levels: responding, preventing, upgrading, experimenting, and creating (Figure 1-1). These levels vary, in part, according to the degree of proactivity each represents. Teams that solely are reactive will spend all their time repairing what is not working. Teams that have become more aggressive in their pursuit of improvement will allocate time to experiment and to create.

Most teams, especially intact work teams and management teams, have some freedom to *discover* and select their own improvement opportunities. The key to continuous improvement rests in precisely this proactive stance toward improvement. Whether improvement opportunities are forced on teams, assigned, or selected, and regardless of the level of opportunity they represent, all opportunities must be transformed into actions, i.e., they must be turned into projects. The first requirement in designing a project is to understand the improvement opportunity or problem.

Understanding an opportunity or problem requires the following steps:

1. Reduce the problem to concrete, manageable dimensions; and
2. Select possible improvement targets.

The starting point for all improvement projects is the Model for Continuous Improvement and Measurement. Problems or opportunities typically will fall into one of the following four categories: team development, customer satisfaction, work processes, and supplier performance. Many of the TQM tools that I have described above can be used to further understand and refine these opportunities and problems (Figure 3-1).

For example, by using one of the rational/structured tools such as brainstorming or the nominal group technique, a team can identify its specific internal and external customers and rank them in order of relative importance. The team then can develop a set of "satisfiers" for each of its customers to track levels of satisfaction.

Or, to use another example, suppose a team decides to reduce the number of customer complaints. It might develop a survey tool to identify what the complaints are and then develop a Pareto chart to understand what problems are complained about the most. Alternatively, this team might use a cause-and-effect diagram to refine its understanding of the causes of customer complaints. Detailed information about improvement projects for customer satisfaction is found in Chapter 5.

Suppose a team decides to work on its own development. One way for it to identify its opportunities is to use a survey tool such as the Superior Team Development Inventory (Kinlaw, 1991; see Appendix) by which it can compare itself to superior teams and identify potential improvement targets. Or the team might use the nominal group technique to identify current opportunities in team development, rank these opportunities by relative importance, and then select an opportunity to work on. More specific information about designing team-development projects is found in Chapter 4.

If a team suspects that a work process can be improved or that it has identified problems in the process, it will first need to develop a flow chart of the process. The flow chart will ensure that the team understands the process before it attempts to adjust it. The flow chart also will force the team to select a portion of the process that is manageable, and it will help the team to develop a coherent plan for improvement rather than a patchwork of unrelated interventions. Next, the team might want to develop one or more control charts to ensure that it is able to separate problems and causes that are special from those that are general and can be attributed to pure chance.

Various TQM tools also can help teams to understand the performance of their suppliers and how to change general problems and opportunities into specific improvement targets. A survey such as the Intergroup Feedback Questionnaire (Kinlaw, 1990; see Appendix) can be used to clarify the working relationships that exist across team boundaries. Teams also can use histograms and run charts to help them to understand data about the input received from their suppliers. These data then can be used to help suppliers to target opportunities for improvement. Improving supplier performance may be as simple as developing a set of mutual team norms through the process of brainstorming.

TQM tools that often are useful during Step 1 are models, brainstorming, the nominal group technique, surveys, flow charts, cause-and-effect diagrams, histograms, control charts, run charts, and scatter diagrams.

Step 2: Define the Specific Improvement Target

The first step in an improvement project is to understand the problems and opportunities. The four broad areas for potential improvement are:

- team development,
- output and customer satisfaction,
- work processes, and
- input and supplier performance.

Figure 2-2 displays each of these four areas as goals and associates with each goal its major improvement strategy.

Within each of these general target areas, there are a multitude of opportunities that will become more specific as the team begins to analyze the target area. For example, within the target of work processes there are, of course, many specific processes. There are processes for producing manufactured products, completing personnel actions, preparing reports, completing experiments, processing insurance claims, and so on. Associated with each process there are an unlimited number of improvement opportunities. As the team analyzes each process, it will discover numerous, specific opportunities for improvement, e.g., shortening the time for a step, eliminating a step, reducing an error, or eliminating the whole process.

The first step in the process of designing improvement projects, understanding an opportunity or problem, often will flow naturally into the second step of the process, identifying specific improvement targets. One reason is that the TQM tools that help teams to understand problems also create data that help teams to identify specific improvement targets.

The collection and analysis of data is the key to identifying specific improvement targets. Data is the raw material that we turn into improvement projects. Data must be the basis for making every decision about improvement.

Data tell us the following:

- our starting point,
- what kind of opportunities we have,
- whether we are getting better or worse, and
- likely causes or goals for improvement.

The Starting Point

Do we want to improve customer satisfaction? What is the starting point? What data do we have about levels of customer satisfaction? What data do we have about which customer satisfiers are most important?

In a moving and storage company, the satisfiers might be: (a) the accuracy of cost estimates, (b) the quality of packing, (c) the quality of storage, (d) the timeliness of delivery, and (e) follow-up by the agent. But which of these satisfiers impact the most on customer satisfaction and ultimate market share?

Do we want to improve one particular process? What data do we have about the process? Is there a predictable spread in the various measures we take of the performance of the process? Is the process under statistical control, i.e., is the difference (the variance) in the measures we take caused by chance or by special causes? What data do we have about total time, time between steps, and error rates?

What Kind of Problem or Opportunity Is It?

A problem or opportunity is a variation of some kind. It is the difference between what exists and what we want to exist or expect to exist. A problem or opportunity also may be what blocks us from getting what we want. The first kind of problem is the *observed variation*. The second kind of problem is the *cause* of the variation. To change a variation, we must address its causes. Improvement projects will remain at the reactive level (Figure 1-1) until they are directed at causes.

Causes come in two forms. There are *random* causes and *special* causes. Random causes are part of any system. If we roll a die enough times, we will get a "one" one-sixth of the times, a "two" one-sixth of the times, a "three" one-sixth of the times, etc. The frequency with which we get one of the numbers is built into the system. If we want to get "ones" more often, we must change the system, i.e., add more "ones" than the other numbers or "load" the die.

Suppose that, after one hundred trials with our die, we end up with "twos" half the time. This occurrence of twos would be three times greater than we could reasonably expect. Now we have a change in frequency that is due to a special cause, e.g., the die is loaded, the roller is cheating, the table is not level, etc.

A driver picks up materials from the warehouse and drops them off at the wrong job. Does this observed variation (incorrect delivery) belong to the system? Can we expect our present delivery system to produce so many incorrect deliveries per month or per year? Is the observed variation attributable to random causes and a chance event such as a "one" turning up on a die? Or is the observed variation attributable to a special cause, a rare event that does not fall within the performance that we can reasonably expect of our delivery system? Only data can give us the answers.

Data can tell us if an event is what we can expect from chance. Data can tell us if our work system is performing as well as we have any right to expect. Data can tell us what kind of problem we have.

The final goal in continuous improvement is to remove *all* error, but until we know what kind of error we have, we cannot know what to do. If our observed variations are from random causes, we can improve our performance only by changing the system. If our observed variations are because of special causes, we can address just these causes without changing the whole system.

Is It Getting Better or Worse?

In the example of the wrong delivery, do we have a positive or negative trend? Are we getting better or worse? The data from run charts can tell us how the frequency of any event is changing.

What Are the Most Likely Causes?

What are the possible reasons that our driver delivered the materials to the wrong job? Some might be: wrong job on invoice, wrong address on invoice, more than one job at same address, materials stacked in truck in wrong order, incorrect verbal directions from dispatcher, and delivery made at end of work day without sufficient time. We can decide which of these are the major causes only after we have determined the frequency of each kind of error.

TQM tools that often are useful during Step 2 are flow charts, Pareto charts, cause-and-effect diagrams, histograms, and scatter diagrams.

Step 3: Design Strategies To Reach the Target

Once an opportunity or problem has been understood and a specific target has been identified, the third step in the design of improvement projects is to determine how we will attack the target. What are our strategies?

Let us assume that a team has looked at its company's process for authorizing travel. Suppose that the team has completed Steps 1 and 2, i.e., developed a flow chart of the process, collected sample data about the performance of the process, etc. Suppose further that the team's improvement target is to reduce by 25 percent the average time it takes to complete all the paper work required to authorize an employee to travel at company expense. The team is now ready to select its strategy.

The team may find that it first must *standardize* the process, that there really is not one process but many. Requests for travel are handled differently in different parts of the company. The team may find that there is some variation in the forms that are used and that special forms have been introduced by certain managers.

The team may decide that it wants to *tighten* the process by eliminating steps or operations or by shortening the time that it takes to complete them. One team that actually looked at this process in its company reduced the steps, operations, and total time by eliminating all signatures that were not truly necessary. Another team reduced the time for a part received on the loading dock to be "binned"—ready to be issued—by eliminating all unnecessary inspections. Unnecessary or "non-value-added" actions in a process are ones that do not complete or improve the service or product.

Suppose an engineering design team decides to reduce the number of amendments that have to be made to a drawing after it has been delivered to the customer. Once it has identified the types of changes that are made and their causes, it decides that its improvement target is to eliminate amendments caused by changes in the customer's requirements or desires. The team may select from several strategies or combinations of strategies. It may revise the way in which design reviews are conducted or it may increase the number of contacts among the engineers and draftspersons and their customers.

Whenever possible, it always is useful to use a single strategy or action to improve quality. This permits the team to assess whether the strategy made a difference and, if so, how much.

TQM tools that often are useful during Step 3 are models, brainstorming, the nominal group technique, and cause-and-effect diagrams.

Step 4: Design the Data Links To Track Performance and To Anticipate Necessary Adjustments

Data links permit teams to monitor performance. Links should exist between the team and the context of team development, between the team and its processes, between the team and its customers, and between the team and its suppliers. These links have two loops. One loop is *initiating* and the other is *receiving*.

Data links are required in order to track each improvement project.

Suppose that a team decides to create a way to reduce the number of tools that are reported lost. It designs a new tagging and tracking system. In order to know the results of its "experiment," it must design a feedback link that gives it the needed data. Once a strategy is selected to handle a problem, the team must track the performance of the strategy.

The technology for measurement and data collection includes devices that are mechanical, electronic, pneumatic, and optical. Data can be retrieved as counts, measurements, reports, and observations.

Data links should be designed with the following criteria in mind:

- Deliver data in time to permit effective action;
- Deliver data in a form that easily is understood by the user;
- Be complete enough to give practical guidance; and
- Be easy to implement and manage.

These criteria will be met if teams respond to the following questions and assign responsibilities for the answers:

- How will the data be collected?
- When will the data be collected?
- Who will collect the data?
- In what form will the data be maintained and reported?
- When will the data be reported?
- To whom will the data be reported?

A variety of mechanical, electronic, pneumatic, and optical devices can be used as data links. In addition, surveys, direct observations, and interviews are useful. Data may be displayed as run charts, control charts, histograms, and the like.

Step 5: Design the Response Process To Use Data from the Data Links

Many organizations spend a lot of time and money surveying their employees but do not implement a strategy *before* conducting the survey to ensure that the data will be used. It is not uncommon for employees to fill out a survey and then to receive little or no information about the results of the survey or any follow-up actions.

A team must include in its improvement project a plan to ensure that there is a process for responding to and using the data that it retrieves. Such a plan will include a statement of *who* is responsible for using the data and *the ways* in which the data will be used.

A work team that provides assistance to all computer users within its company decided to track the time that elapsed between the receipt of a call for assistance and the time that the internal customer indicated that the problem was solved. The team determined that the most pervasive reason for a delay in the closeout of a request for help was that some people on the team were considered to be experts on certain systems and other members were considered to be experts on other systems. The result was that customers had to wait for help until the "right" expert was available. Work loads, authorized absences, and vacations made it unlikely that an expert on one particular system always would be available to take care of customers with questions about that system. The team decided to make all its members competent in all the computer systems used by the company and undertook a major cross-training program.

As cross-training proceeded, the team monitored on a weekly basis the average time it took to close out customers' requests. One person on the team was responsible for the whole project. Another person was responsible for retrieving the data about closeout time. This same person was responsible for carrying out the uses that the team wanted to make of the data. These uses were:

- To provide the team with a weekly update of average closeout times and trends;
- To let the team know the systems for which customers were requesting help most frequently; and
- To use the data to adjust the team members' schedules and priorities for cross-training.

TQM tools that often are useful during Step 5 are Pareto charts, histograms, run charts, and control charts.

Step 6: Determine How the Project Will Be Managed

The final step in designing improvement projects is to determine how the project will be managed. This step requires that teams ensure the following:

- One team member has overall responsibility for the project;
- All other key responsibilities have been assigned;
- Milestones for the project are established;

- Progress of the project is reported regularly;
- Resources are available for the project; and
- Sufficient records of the project are kept.

The team is, of course, ultimately responsible for all its improvement projects. Each project should, however, have a single person who is charged with ensuring that the team's design is carried out. The role of this person will rarely be as formal as that of project manager. The person responsible for the project typically will do things such as:

- Stay current about every aspect of the project;
- Help the team to meet the project's milestones;
- Keep the team aware of the project's progress, results, and problems; and
- Keep records of the project for the team.

Tools that often are useful in this phase of a project are project-management sheets and milestone charts. Examples of these are found in the Appendix.

SUMMARY

In this chapter, I have discussed the characteristics of improvement projects, the critical role that data play in improvement projects, and the six steps for designing improvement projects. I also have given a brief description of the TQM tools that teams are likely to use to design and undertake significant improvement projects. In the following chapters, I will describe improvement projects related to the four major opportunities for improvement: team development, customer satisfaction, work processes, and supplier performance.

Chapter 4

*Improving and Measuring the
Context of Team Development*

The Model for Continuous Improvement and Measurement indicates that there are four major areas of opportunity in which teams can improve the quality of their own performance and that of their organizations. These areas are:

- the context of *team development* within which the team functions;
- the team's *output* and *customer satisfaction;*
- *work processes;* and
- *input* to the team and *supplier performance.*

Figure 2-2 displays these four areas and their primary improvement strategies in parallel. It is clear that teams and organizations must pursue continuous improvement in all these areas. However, the very first step that every team must take toward continuous improvement is to improve its own ability to function as a team. Continuous improvement begins with team development and it can be sustained only by highly developed work teams. Improvement projects in the areas of customer satisfaction, work processes, and supplier performance can be designed and implemented successfully only by work groups that are able to function as teams. Research (Kinlaw, 1991) indicates that superior performance is the product of superior teams, and the better the team, the better will be the improvement projects. Organizations that are willing to settle for less than superior teams inevitably are accepting less than superior performance and improvement.

Team development should be supported by the purposefulness and conscious direction that is characteristic of improvement in any of the four major areas. Projects in team development should, therefore, have the characteristics of all improvement projects. They should be:

- team-centered and team-driven,
- structured and systematic,
- biased toward proactivity,
- based on data and measurable, and
- long-term in emphasis.

It may appear redundant to suggest that team development is team-centered and team-driven. But the fact of the matter is that many managers, supervisors, and other key people in organizations still think of leadership as directing, decision-making, or controlling in one form or another, so they often approach team development in the same way that they have approached all their other tasks in the past. They will try, by themselves, to figure out what their work groups need to do to develop into teams.

I run about a hundred workshops a year that are concerned with team development. One of the recurring questions that I hear from managers and supervisors is "What do I do next?" The answer is, of course, "Ask your team." *Teams develop teams.* The very best teams are ones in which every member has assumed responsibility for the team's development.

Saying that teams develop teams does not mean that managers, supervisors, and other institutional leaders should not take the initiative in team development. It is clear that the dominant role emerging for managers and supervisors is that of developers of teams. It also is clear that this is a role in which most managers and supervisors are not comfortable.

In a previous book (Kinlaw, 1991), I describe the roles and responsibilities of team leaders. A quotation from that earlier work suggests what team leadership is.

> Leadership in superior work teams is radically different from the way leadership is traditionally understood. In its most general terms, leadership is described as the process of gaining followers. The logic is that to be a leader, one must have followers. Leadership requires "followership." This kind of logic immediately presents problems for understanding leadership in superior work teams. Leadership in superior teams does not mean creating followers. It means being a team player and creating team players.

The purpose of this chapter is to develop guidelines for designing projects in team development. In the pages that follow, I will use the steps for designing an improvement project and suggest how teams can design their own team-development projects.

STEP 1: UNDERSTAND THE OPPORTUNITY OR PROBLEM

As with all other improvement projects, team development can be initiated at any level of opportunity from responding to creating (Figure 1-1). An improvement project may be initiated because the team has become aware of a problem or because the team has established team development as one of its improvement opportunities. The discussion that follows will not make a distinction between the five levels of improvement opportunities.

To understand our opportunities for team development, we must answer two questions:

- When and where do teams exist?
- How do teams become superior teams?

When and Where Do Teams Exist?

A potential team exists whenever two or more people join together in order to do work. A team exists whenever and wherever two or more people decide to be a team. As I use the word team, therefore, I have in mind every conceivable opportunity for two or more people to improve any aspect of the performance of their jobs, of their team, and of their larger organization.

One of the mistakes that organizations make is to use the word "team" to apply only to a special group of people who have been joined together for a special purpose. The rise and fall of quality circles can be attributed largely to this. Many organizations are approaching TQM with the same team strategy that they used with quality circles, i.e., insisting that TQM will be supported by TQM teams, and that for teams to qualify as TQM teams, they must be special teams set aside to work *only* on a particular work process.

By applying "team" only to special groups and by placing their primary emphasis on such teams, organizations are working against their own best interests and are ensuring that continuous improvement will not become part of their natural way of doing business. By emphasizing special teams, organizations create the following problems:

- They communicate the message that teamwork and team development are special activities that are the concern of special people;
- They set up the dysfunctional expectation that to be a team member and a team player, one has to leave one's usual work group;
- They draw attention away from the primary unit of productivity in which continuous improvement must be institutionalized: the natural work group;
- They create a parallel organization of special teams that easily will come into conflict with the regular organization over things such as time, people, and other resources; and

- They fail to equip the most important set of potential team leaders—their supervisors and managers—for their new roles as the developers of teams.

Teams can vary in at least the following ways:

- Whether they are the usual work teams within the normal organizational structure or whether they have been formed for a special reason;
- Whether the membership is voluntary or involuntary;
- Whether their improvement opportunities are assigned or whether the team has the freedom to identify them;
- Whether they cross internal organizational boundaries or whether they exist within a single work unit;
- Whether they cross external organizational boundaries or whether they exist within the same company; and
- Whether they are self-managed or have an assigned leader.

Special teams must, of course, be created to attack special opportunities for improvement. But every team should be engaged in continuous improvement, and every group of people in the organization must learn to think of itself as a team. There is no end to the number of possibilities for people to be joined together as teams. Some of the ways in which teams can and do exist are as:

1. **Intact Work Teams.** These are groups of people who work together daily and who, most often, have a supervisor or leader. They also may be *self-managing teams.*

2. **Management Teams.** These are teams composed of a manager and his or her staff and direct reports, including secretaries, deputies, technical assistants, etc.

3. **Interface Teams**. These are composed of groups that must work together across an organizational boundary to get the job done. Interface teams may exist within the same organization, e.g., between design engineering and manufacturing, and between different organizations. They include *customer-supplier teams* and *supplier-customer teams.*

4. **Project Teams.** These are groups that are created in order to complete a specific task within a designated period of time. Examples are design teams, procurement teams, flight project teams, and construction teams.

5. **Special-Improvement Teams.** These teams have all sorts of titles and descriptions. They have been called quality-action teams, process-improvement teams, cross-functional teams, quality-management teams, and the like.

6. **Network Teams.** Often people work together, share information, and participate in related tasks but rarely see one another. Most of their business is transacted by means of the telephone, electronic mail, or paper. An example is the network of secretaries that link together various processes and actions in organizations.

7. **Committees and Councils.** These include all the permanent and temporary groups such as EEO councils, source-evaluation boards, awards committees, child-care committees, and promotion boards.

Opportunities for team development first begin to present themselves when we recognize the unlimited number of opportunities that we have to be teams. Opportunities next present themselves when we ask, "What are the key strategies for developing into a superior team?"

How Do Teams Become Superior Teams?

There are a number of very useful and straightforward strategies for developing superior teams. Four such strategies are discussed below.

Establish Team Norms

Groups cannot become teams, and teams cannot become superior teams, without norms. Norms are the written or unwritten rules that govern the behavior of team members. Norms can develop over time without conscious intention; they become embedded in the culture of an organization or team. They become the "recognized" ways of doing things. Norms also can be developed intentionally. They can be made explicit and can describe how team members want to behave, not how they currently behave. In this latter instance, the norms become improvement targets.

Norms that govern the way in which a work team intends to function can address such variables as:

- How will feedback on performance be given? Will supervisors receive feedback from other team members as well as give feedback to them?
- What is expected in terms of the responsiveness of team members to one another? Are members expected to give as much priority to the work of their colleagues as they do to their own?
- What about privileges? Will some team members use reserved parking if all members do not have it?
- What are the expectations about dealing with conflict and speaking one's mind? Can this be done safely?
- What is expected in regard to the quality of service and products delivered to internal and external customers?
- How will the team handle awards? Will it insist on team awards rather than individual ones?

These are only a few of the issues that norms address and for which clear expectations for team members' behavior should be established.

Rating the Team Against Superior Teams

There are four sets of characteristics that distinguish superior teams; any team can use them to rate team development and to identify improvement opportunities (Kinlaw, 1991). They are as follows:

1. **Team Results.** Superior teams consistently achieve the following: maximum use of people, delivery of superior services and products in the face of every conceivable difficulty, continuous improvement, and enthusiastically positive customers.

2. **Informal Processes.** Superior teams create and make extensive use of informal processes such as communicating and contacting, responding and adapting, influencing and improving, and appreciating and celebrating.

3. **Positive Team Feelings.** Members of superior teams typically share feelings of inclusion, commitment, loyalty, pride, and trust.

4. **Leadership.** The leaders of superior teams fulfill the following roles: initiator, model, and coach.

These sets of characteristics can be used with various TQM tools (e.g., brainstorming, nominal group technique, cause-and-effect diagrams) to clarify opportunities and to identify specific improvement targets. One particularly powerful tool that can be used to identify improvement opportunities and develop a baseline of team development is a survey based on the four sets of superior team characteristics. A sample of such a survey (*The Superior Team Development Survey*, Part 4) is found in the Appendix.

Figure 4-1 is a list of improvement targets that were developed by one team. The team used the nominal group technique to create a weighted list of ways to strengthen the sense of appreciation among its members.

Figure 4-2 (page 84) is an example from a team that used a cause-and-effect diagram to help it understand what caused members to feel that they were not included.

Evaluate Team Meetings

A third strategy for team development is for the team to evaluate its team meetings. Teams are not just teams when they meet—

```
┌─────────────────────────────────────────────────────────┐
│                                                         │
│        Opportunities Listed in Order of Importance      │
│                                                         │
│   1. Set aside time at each team meeting to acknowledge special │
│      achievements of team members.                      │
│   2. Identify major milestones or goals and, when they are reached, │
│      have a team celebration.                           │
│   3. Invite senior managers to team meetings to let them know what │
│      the team is doing.                                 │
│   4. Create a reward for the person who gets stuck with the dirtiest │
│      or most uninteresting jobs.                        │
│   5. Make sure the team takes advantage of all the formal awards │
│      offered by the company.                            │
│                                                         │
└─────────────────────────────────────────────────────────┘
```

Figure 4-1. Team Opportunities To Improve Appreciation, Developed by Using Nominal Group Technique

although much of what is written about teams focuses only on this aspect of a team's life. Team meetings do, however, provide teams with a special opportunity for improvement. Teams must meet periodically to solve problems and to identify opportunities for improvement through the kinds of communication and interaction that can be accomplished only in face-to-face conversations. Three major variables determine the effectiveness and efficiency of team meetings (Kinlaw, 1991). These variables are *resources, structure,* and *communication.*

Resources include things such as the team's:

- Having access to the information required;

- Having the facilities and equipment for the meeting;

- Having the necessary time to conduct the meeting;

- Having the financial resources to support team decisions; and

- Having the right people at the meeting.

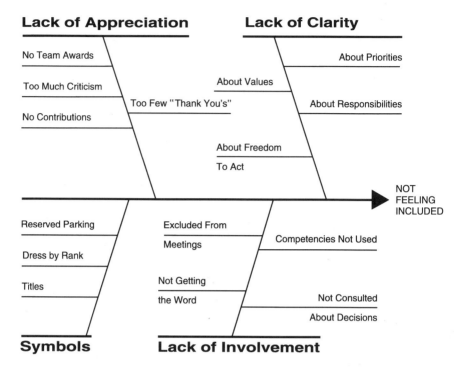

Lack of Appreciation

No Team Awards

Too Much Criticism

No Contributions

Too Few "Thank You's"

Lack of Clarity

About Priorities

About Values

About Responsibilities

About Freedom

To Act

NOT FEELING INCLUDED

Reserved Parking

Dress by Rank

Titles

Excluded From

Meetings

Not Getting

the Word

Competencies Not Used

Not Consulted

About Decisions

Symbols

Lack of Involvement

Figure 4-2. Team-Development Opportunities, Identified by Using a Cause-and-Effect Diagram

Structure includes:

- Clarity about the roles and responsibilities of members;
- Having agreed-on norms that cover such things as when to start, when to end, how decisions will be made, how to deal with subgrouping and interruptions, how members are expected to participate, and how conflict will be managed;
- Having a clear agenda/goals/objectives;
- Using rational/structured TQM tools; and
- Evaluating team meetings regularly.

Communication includes the skills of members in listening, developing information, and avoiding the behaviors that block inquiry. The subject of inquiry is discussed later in this book.

There are two simple tools for teams to use in evaluating and improving their team meetings: the use of norms and the use of a questionnaire or survey.

Norms for meetings can be developed by using brainstorming or the nominal group technique. Figure 4-3 is a set of instructions that I regularly use in one of my TQM seminars to help participating groups to develop norms that they will use during the seminar. Figure 4-4 (page 87) is an example of a typical set of norms that teams develop for their meetings.

Figure 4-5 (page 88) is an example of a survey that teams can use periodically to evaluate their meetings. Teams can keep track of their performance by summarizing the data from the survey and displaying them as bar charts and run charts.

Individual Team-Member Feedback

A fourth effective tool for team development is for each team member to receive feedback on a regular basis from the other team members. For feedback among team members to be effective, it must be established as a team norm. Also, the way in which feedback is given must be part of the team norms.

Feedback among team members should have the following characteristics:

1. First, and most important, feedback must stimulate and support team development. *Feedback as a team-development tool must always focus on behaviors that are associated with being superior team members.* The team should not concern itself with individual growth. Its concern should be with the growth of the team.

2. Feedback should be about behaviors for which the entire team has agreed-on norms and which all team members believe should characterize every team member's performance.

TEAM ACTIVITY AND EVALUATION

Return to the general session at_____o'clock.

Tasks:

1. Use the brainstorming technique. Develop and record a set of norms for your meetings during the seminar, i.e., what you will expect about member participation; how members are expected to interact and participate; how you will make decisions; how you will resolve conflict; how you will share leadership; what you will expect about timeliness; how you will record your discussions, findings, plans; etc. Be sure to record your group norms. You will use these norms periodically to evaluate your team's performance. Use the space below and the back of this sheet to record these norms.

Team Norms:

2. Discuss the following questions and record your responses.

   • Describe what you understand to be the key elements in your company's (or organization's) Total Quality Management Program. What direct effect has this program had on your work team?

   • What (if any) have been some specific improvements that your team has achieved in the last six months?

3. After you have developed responses to question 2, use the team norms that you have developed and evaluate your session. Revise or add to your norms as you discover new values or behaviors that should be clarified.

4. Designate someone to present the following at the general session:

   • The team norms that you developed;

   • The effect of your norms on your team's discussion.

Figure 4-3. Instructions for Developing Norms for Team Meetings

```
• Don't criticize
• Don't interrupt
• Stay focused on the task
• Everyone participates fully
• Make all decisions by consensus
• Establish up front what we are doing and the time for each part
• Rotate leadership of team
• Use a timer to keep us on schedule
• Develop each person's input fully
• Avoid nitpicking
• Evaluate our performance at the end of each team meeting
```

Figure 4-4. Example of Norms for Team Meetings

3. Feedback should be specific and concrete, so that it clearly describes the appreciated behaviors or desired improvement.

4. Feedback should be given according to a process that is approved by the entire team.

The way in which feedback is given will depend on the level of trust and comfort that has been achieved in the team. Nonetheless, the process for giving feedback always should be structured and standardized, i.e., every team member should receive feedback in relation to the same set of variables or characteristics.

A team can designate particular meetings in which members will give personal feedback to one another. If time allows, each individual member can have a private session with every other member. The team can use a written instrument that is completed on a regular basis by each member in regard to every other member.

My experience suggests that there are four key characteristics of members of superior teams: *listening, responding, including,* and

First, each team member should take a few minutes to complete the *Team Evaluation Sheet.* Then the team should discuss each item on the evaluation sheet and identify and record opportunities for improvement.

TEAM EVALUATION SHEET

	Completely Agree						*Do Not Agree At All*
1. Everyone is involved and active.	7	6	5	4	3	2	1
2. We listen to one another.	7	6	5	4	3	2	1
3. No one dominates the discussions.	7	6	5	4	3	2	1
4. We understand our team's tasks.	7	6	5	4	3	2	1
5. We stay focused on our tasks.	7	6	5	4	3	2	1
6. We develop clear procedures or steps for performing our tasks.	7	6	5	4	3	2	1
7. We distribute responsibilities equally.	7	6	5	4	3	2	1
8. We generate creative ideas.	7	6	5	4	3	2	1
9. We move efficiently toward our objectives without getting bogged down.	7	6	5	4	3	2	1
10. We treat one another with respect.	7	6	5	4	3	2	1
11. We don't have any issues to resolve that affect our team's performance.	7	6	5	4	3	2	1

OPPORTUNITIES FOR TEAM IMPROVEMENT:

Figure 4-5. Team-Meeting Evaluation Survey

appreciating. Figure 4-6 (page 90) is a feedback tool that permits team members to evaluate one another in regard to these four behaviors.

STEP 2: DEFINE THE SPECIFIC IMPROVEMENT TARGET

I will use the example concerning team members' feelings of not being included from Step 1 to illustrate the remaining steps in designing a team-development improvement project.

From the various causes that the team associated with the feeling of not being included, it first selected "not getting the information we need." The team reworked the cause in order to turn it into an improvement target, which was "to reduce to zero the number of complaints that members have about not having the information they need." The team's next step was to select its strategies for reaching this target.

STEP 3: DESIGN STRATEGIES TO REACH THE TARGET

The team used brainstorming to generate the strategies that it would use to reach its improvement target. The set of strategies that it finally selected was:

- Hold ten-minute, stand-up meeting at 8:05 each morning in which each person describes his/her priorities and problems (if any);
- Each Friday afternoon, supervisor to issue a list of the decisions and actions taken during the week that might affect the team or any member of the team; and
- Each team member to use the grid in Figure 4-7 (page 91) to ensure that every other team member is advised when he/she takes any action that affects other members.

	Very Typical				Not Typical At All

Member Receiving Feedback: _____ Date:_____

Member Giving Feedback: _____Period Covered:_____

	Very Typical				Not Typical At All

Listening

1. Pays close attention when I
   speak to her/him.   5   4   3   2   1

2. Helps me to clarify what I am
   trying to say.   5   4   3   2   1

Responding

3. Is quick to give help when
   I ask for it.   5   4   3   2   1

4. Fulfills commitments to
   me on time.   5   4   3   2   1

Involving

5. Ensures that I am included in
   decisions that affect me.   5   4   3   2   1

6. Asks for my input in areas of
   my competencies.   5   4   3   2   1

Appreciating

7. Is quick to thank me for
   my efforts.   5   4   3   2   1

8. Makes a point of letting others
   know about my achievements.   5   4   3   2   1

Figure 4-6. Team-Member Feedback Sheet

Team Member:_____ Period of Report:_____

Action Taken	Team Member Affected	Informed?		Notes
		Yes	No	

Figure 4-7. Information-Sharing Chart

STEP 4: DESIGN THE DATA LINKS

The team in our example decided to use the following data links:

- Canvas each member each Friday for a self-report of each instance in which he/she did not receive needed information; and

- Canvas each member each Friday for a self-report of each instance in which he/she recognized an instance in which he/she should have given some information to another member but failed to do so.

The data were collected and reported in the following ways:

1. A run chart (Figure 4-8) showing the total number of times during a week that members experienced not getting the information they needed (not getting information in time counted as not getting it).

Improving the Context of Team Development

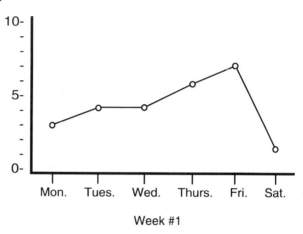

Team Member: _____

Period of Report: _____

Times information
not received

Figure 4-8. Run Chart for Times Information Not Received

2. A run chart (Figure 4-9) showing the total number of times during a week that members recognized that they did not give information to another member that they should have given (not given in time counted as not given).

3. Bar charts (Figure 4-10, page 94) for each week, showing comparisons of the number of times members reported not receiving information and the number of times members reported not giving information.

STEP 5: DESIGN THE RESPONSE PROCESS TO USE DATA FROM THE DATA LINKS

One team member was given the responsibility of retrieving the data. This member was to report the data in the form agreed on

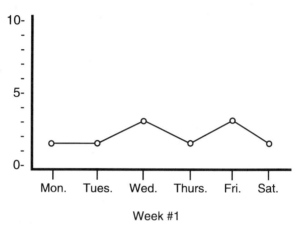

Team Member: _____

Period of Report: _____

Times information
not shared.

Week #1

Figure 4-9. Run Chart For Times Information Not Shared

(Step 4) at the team's weekly TQM meeting. The whole team assumed responsibility for responding to the data.[1]

STEP 6: DETERMINE HOW THE PROJECT WILL BE MANAGED

The design for managing the project included the following:

- Overall Responsibility. The project was not complex, so the same person who was responsible for collecting the data

---

[1]The effect of tracking the perceptions of members of when they did not receive information and when they did not share information was to increase members' sensitivity to the need to share information and to help them recognize that they typically over-estimated how much information they actually shared.

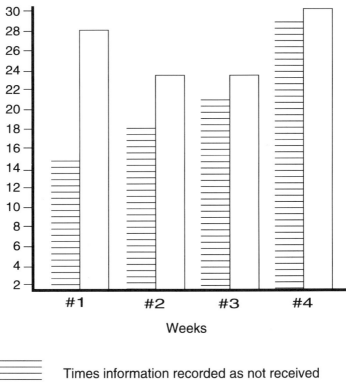

Times information recorded as not received

Times information recorded as not shared

**Figure 4-10. Bar Chart Comparing Times Information
Not Received and Times Information Not Shared**

assumed overall responsibility for the project. There were
no other key responsibilities in the project.

- Milestones. The team identified the following milestones:
  date on which data first would be retrieved, date on which
  data first would be reported, and period of time that project
  would run before being modified or canceled.

- **Progress of the Project.** To be reported weekly at the team's TQM meeting.

- **Resources.** The member who was responsible for the project was requested to keep a record of the time spent on the project and to report to the team any problem with time or other resources.

- **Records.** Records to be kept included data from run charts and bar charts, minutes from discussions of the project at team TQM meetings, and a summary of the project at close out.

SUMMARY

Team-development projects can be initiated because teams become aware of problems that interfere with the members' ability to do business. Opportunities for team development occur when teams actively set out to be superior teams. Opportunities for team development immediately begin to present themselves when we:

- Become aware of the unlimited number of opportunities that are available for team formation and improvement;

- Rate our own teams against the standards set by superior teams; and

- Regularly evaluate our team meetings.

In this chapter, I have discussed how to design team-development improvement projects. In the next chapter, I will discuss how to design projects for improving output and customer satisfaction.

Chapter 5

Improving and Measuring Output and Customer Satisfaction

The overarching TQM *strategy* is continuous improvement in team development and performance. Continuous improvement is a team-centered, team-driven process. The overarching *goal* of continuous improvement is customer satisfaction. Customer satisfaction—like every other aspect of improvement—must be continuous if it is to be successful and long-term.

The primary purpose of this chapter is to develop guidelines that teams can use in designing projects to improve output and customer satisfaction. First, however, I would like to discuss three preliminary topics:

- The differences between external and internal customers;
- The meaning of customer satisfaction; and
- How to make customers part of the team.

DIFFERENCES BETWEEN EXTERNAL AND INTERNAL CUSTOMERS

There are two classes of customers: internal customers and external customers. All teams have internal customers. All organizations have external customers. Some teams also have external customers. It is likely that the needs of our internal and external customers will differ and that our relationships with our two kinds of customers will differ. Regardless of these differences in needs and relationships, internal and external customers are linked in one very special way. *The degree to which work teams satisfy their internal customers will have a profound impact on the organization's ability to satisfy its external customers.*

Distinctions between internal and external customers are not exact and these distinctions sometimes break down. Nevertheless, three general distinctions can help us to understand the different kinds of issues that we face in attempting to satisfy these two different classes of customers.

The first distinction is the *degree of freedom* that external and internal customers have. Most of our external customers have the freedom to use or not use our services or products. Our internal customers rarely have such freedom.

The second distinction is that our external customers have *direct power* over our reputation, our profitability, our market share, and, ultimately, our organization's existence; our internal customers may have *little direct power* over us.

The third distinction is that the *payoffs* from satisfying internal customers differ from those of satisfying external customers. Internal customers rarely have the power of the marketplace. They rarely determine if their internal suppliers will continue to exist. Our internal customers do, however, shape the image that we enjoy in the company. Image, in turn, can determine the kind of work that our team is given; it can influence the kind of people who are assigned to us; and it can affect the level of resources that we receive. The more positive the image of a work team is, the more likely it is that it will be assigned interesting work; the more likely it is that it will attract superior people; and the more likely it is that it can compete for resources such as equipment, money, and people. The payoffs for satisfying internal customers are just as real as those for satisfying external customers. The payoffs are simply different.

Individuals and work teams all serve *directly* a variety of *internal customers.* All individuals and work teams serve *indirectly* the organization's *external customers*. Some individuals and work teams also serve *external* customers *directly*. The point is that we all have customers, and what can be observed about internal customers will, to a lesser or greater degree, apply to external customers, and vice versa.

THE MEANING OF CUSTOMER SATISFACTION

Most of us have had a lot of experience in being customers. As I analyze more than five decades of experience in being both an internal and external customer, I conclude that satisfaction as a customer can be reduced to a very simple set of causes. It comes from:

1. Some person or product that contributes to my capacity to perform or to my sense of personal well-being;
2. Knowing that something will work as well as or better than I expected; and
3. Being treated as though I were important.

The preceding three items say nothing about cost or price. Try as I might, I could not recall a single time in which the cost of a product or service (by itself) was the primary reason for my sense of satisfaction or dissatisfaction.

In the case of being an external customer, I can recall many times in which I have been dissatisfied because I have paid for a meal, or a piece of computer software, or a pair of shoes, or the repair of an automobile and have felt very dissatisfied. But the reason for my dissatisfaction was not directly the price. It was that the cost was disproportionate to the value received. The cost for a tasteless meal, or for software that does not work as advertised, or for shoes that bend in an annoying spot, or for a car repair that does not last until I get home is always too much. It has not been primarily the *cost for quality* in a service or product that has bothered me; it has been the *cost for the lack of quality* that has bothered me.

In the case of being an internal customer, I can recall many times in which I have been dissatisfied because the personnel department has not been prompt in helping me to fill a vacancy, or a colleague has failed to provide me with promised data, or a person or group has held me up by failing to make a timely decision, or a form has been unnecessarily long or confusing. Here, again, I have been most bothered by the cost for lack of quality (wasted time and not being able to do my job as well as I wanted to), not by the cost for quality.

As it turns out, my perceptions about satisfaction (at least as an external customer) are supported by a great deal of research. For example, the Profit Impact of Market Strategy (PIMS), a data base that is maintained by the Strategic Planning Institute in Cambridge, Massachusetts, indicates that the one variable that has the most effect on long-term market share is the perceived quality of a service or product. A large-scale study conducted for the American Business Conference concluded that top-performing companies had one practice in common: they did not go after a low-cost, low-end position in the market but focused on producing high-quality, value-added products that often cost more to produce than competing products.

A "quality" phenomenon in the State of Virginia is Ukrop's Super Markets chain. Ukrop's has twenty stores in and around Richmond. In a 1989 survey (Beacon Press, 1989), Ukrop's was undisputedly the leader over every other food chain in market share, income, cleanliness, friendliness, checkout service, and just about every other category. Ukrop's does not have the lowest prices, but its hamburger has less gristle, its seafood is fresher, and the produce sparkles. Price is not what is important at Ukrop's; quality is. Jim Roberts, the editor of *Food World,* has said that Ukrop's probably could raise prices without hurting its business. As one customer put it:

You don't just go to Ukrop's to shop; you go to see your friends. And your friends are there because of Ukrop's quality of product, quality of people—which is extraordinary—and quality of service. (McDonald & James, 1987)

Customer satisfaction, both internal and external, is a function of quality of service, quality of product, and quality of treatment. The achievement and improvement of this kind of satisfaction usually requires that a team reconsider its current level of commitment to satisfy its customers. It certainly means that the team must establish its own operating principles for managing customer satisfaction. Examples of such principles are as follows:

1. Deliver to our customers services and products that are 100 percent fit to use 100 percent of the time.
2. Let everything we do in relation to our customers reflect our belief that they determine our future.
3. Accept our customers as the final judges of the quality of our services and products.
4. Aggressively seek feedback from our customers and accept all feedback from them as potentially useful information.
5. Respond immediately to resolve any problems that our customers have with our services or products.
6. Involve our customers in the process of improving our services and products.
7. Ensure that our customers never have the same problem twice with our services and products.
8. Anticipate the developing and future needs of our customers.

Satisfying External Customers

A few months ago, I called a firm that rents computer hardware and arranged to rent some equipment. I talked to a "technician" and told him exactly what I wanted. I specifically requested that the equipment be tested before I pick it up. I later picked up the equipment, took it to my office, and plugged it in. The computer turned on, but I could make no entry from the keyboard. I did a little trouble shooting, to no avail. I called the firm and was told to bring the equipment back. When I returned the equipment, the technician discovered that I had been given a keyboard that was not compatible with the computer. I spoke to the manager and asked him whether he knew how often rented equipment did not work and the most common reasons. His answer was, "No, I don't. We focus more on servicing our equipment. We always make it right if our customers complain."

I suspect that many of this company's customers, like myself, will quickly learn to look for another supplier who delivers a product that is 100 percent fit to use, not one that is repaired 100 percent of the time *after a customer complains.*

I travel a lot and have become something of an authority on just how poorly many airlines manage customer satisfaction. For example, the service tray comes by, and I ask for coffee with milk. The flight attendant says, "We only have a few cartons of milk and we have to keep them for our milk drinkers." Each time I hear the captain say, "Please sit back, enjoy your trip, and let us know if there is anything we can do to make your flight more enjoyable," I feel like shouting "baloney!" Messages such as this create a sense of incongruity and only increase my sense of not-being-a-customer.

We have a long way to go to satisfy our external customers. I suspect that we have even farther to go to satisfy our internal customers. Having internal customers is not a familiar idea to most people. For example, I use a Total Quality Management Inventory to help teams to assess their current levels of TQM awareness and activity. One set of items is concerned with internal customers. The feedback that I often receive from teams is, "We don't have any internal customers."

Satisfying Internal Customers

In the organizations about which I have reliable information, it is very unlikely that work teams regard "satisfying their internal customers" as a significant part of their jobs. Most work teams have not identified their internal customers, much less started specific projects to increase the satisfaction of their internal customers.

In my work with organizations, I have been able to observe some events that occur with such frequency that they can be classified. These events fall into three dominant classes:

- lack of responsiveness,
- misinformation, and
- lack of listening and feedback.

These behaviors are common in the way in which we respond to both our external and internal customers, but they may be more unconscious with our internal customers.

Lack of Responsiveness

Responsiveness to internal customers often falls on a scale of from little to none. Consider the following common experience.

Employee A calls group X to receive some technical information from employee B. Employee A is told that employee B is not at work and that there is no one else who can help employee A. The costs of this lack of responsiveness may consist of any or all of the following:

- The time that the call takes is wasted for employee A and for the person who answered it but did not help;
- Other events depend on employee A's getting the information from employee B, and the result is a queuing effect with its attendant losses in time and productivity;
- Employee A has to take a variety of time-consuming actions to work around the fact that the information from employee B is not available;
- The requested information is useful for a specific window of opportunity; once the window is closed, the opportunity is gone.

We are not being responsive when we fail to help our internal customers get the information they need. We also are not being responsive when we become more concerned about rules than about the success of our internal customers.

A finance group is in the midst of an end-of-year audit and is operating against an almost impossible deadline. A desktop computer that one of its employees is using develops a problem. The employee tries to get a temporary replacement but is told that she must get her supervisor's authorization. The supervisor is at a meeting in corporate headquarters. The employee finally chases down the manager of her department to get the necessary authorization. The manager becomes furious about being bothered with so trivial a problem but authorizes the replacement. Because no one viewed the employee as a valued customer and responded quickly to help her get a replacement for her computer, the employee wasted time, her manager wasted time, and work on the audit was delayed.

Lack of responsiveness is evident when people and work teams fail to meet schedules and commitments. It is evident when people waste others' time making excuses or listing the reasons that they did not fulfill a request.

Misinformation

Another indication that we do not view other people and groups internal to our organizations as customers is the prevalence of misinformation. People rarely tell outright lies to their internal customers, but they do "avoid" telling the whole truth.

By a certain date, Group A is supposed to have the input for a report that Group B is preparing. The date passes, and Group A inquires about the input. Group B responds with a number of excuses without telling Group A the whole truth (e.g., it hasn't started to prepare the input; it has messed up the input; it doesn't have the resources to put together the input; etc.). The result is that Group A continues to operate on the assumption that it will get the input it needs (which it may not), and we have the possibility of a future catastrophe because Group B did not treat Group A as a valued customer.

Lack of Listening and Feedback

A necessary corollary to the fact that most people and most teams in most organizations do not view their colleagues and fellow teams as customers is that they do not listen to and receive feedback from their colleagues and fellow teams. Listening is, of course, one form of feedback. I use it with feedback as a matter of emphasis and to draw attention to the need to obtain feedback through personal contact as well as through more formal methods.

If we do not accept the idea that we have internal customers, we certainly will not perceive the need to solicit feedback from them. The absence of feedback is probably as good an indicator as we have that "internal customer" is an idea that has yet to catch on in an organization.

Without feedback from their internal customers, teams isolate themselves in their own self-constructed images and remain untouched (and untroubled) by data. They, instead of their customers, become the final arbiters of the quality of their services and products.

If design engineering does not view fabrication and manufacturing as its customers, it can persist in the wasteful games of faulting them for delays and mistakes in the way in which designs are interpreted. If a metrology and calibration laboratory does not view the instrumentation and test groups as customers, it will not use complaints as opportunities for possible improvement but will go out of its way to prove that the user groups introduced error into the instruments after they were recertified by metrology and calibration.

HOW TO MAKE CUSTOMERS PART OF THE TEAM

It clearly is to the advantage of suppliers to include their customers on their teams. A supplier's goal should be to involve its customers fully in helping the supplier to improve its services and products. There are many ways in which to include customers on the supplier's team. Some of them are:

1. Develop a feedback process to measure customer satisfaction. By developing a process *with* its customers, a supplier naturally begins to build better teamwork.

2. Initiate special problem-solving and improvement teams with customers.

3. Develop creative ways to express appreciation to customers.

4. Initiate mutual planning sessions with customers to ensure that the supplier is able to anticipate and support changes in customers' needs.

5. Maintain continual personal contact and interaction with customers at all levels of the organization.

6. Offer to customers the supplier's own experience and technology in total quality management.

There are no limits to the number of ways in which suppliers can engage in teamwork with their customers. The most important step that suppliers can take is to think of their customers as potential team members. Once suppliers set team development with their customers as a goal, many strategies become obvious. The most obvious strategy is for suppliers to declare their intentions and then let their customers help them determine how to develop better teamwork.

Customer satisfaction, like all other targets in continuous improvement, is achieved and enhanced through specific projects. The remainder of this chapter will describe how teams can design projects to improve customer satisfaction.

STEP 1: UNDERSTAND THE OPPORTUNITY OR PROBLEM

To understand opportunities for improving customer satisfaction, we must know the following:

- Who are our customers?;

- What is the measured quality of our services and products?;
- What are our customers' perceptions of our output, i.e., our services and products?; and
- What are our customers' expectations of our output?

Who Are Our Customers?

Improving customer satisfaction begins with identifying the team's internal and external customers. The next step is to determine if there is any reason to set priorities for tracking or improving customer satisfaction, i.e., are there current problems or opportunities for certain customers that should be addressed first? One of the rational/structured tools such as brainstorming or the nominal group technique can be used in this effort.

Usually, teams will identify individuals and teams that they previously did not think of as customers. Technicians and mechanics begin to recognize their quality inspectors as their internal customers; personnel officers begin to perceive their recruits and newly hired employees as customers; and engineers begin to think of their draftspersons as customers.

By thinking systematically about their customers, teams not only develop clarity about who their customers are but they also may understand better the relative importance of their customers. As George Orwell might have observed, "All customers are equal, but some are more equal than others."

A team that was responsible for designing new equipment to transport and store liquid oxygen and hydrogen came to a new understanding of the relative importance of its customers. This team was part of a larger organization that had a contract with NASA. NASA was the final user of the team's services and products. NASA evaluated the team's performance and ultimately paid for the team's services through a support-services contract. It was natural that the team viewed NASA as its most important customer.

Once the team listed all of its internal customers and all the services and products that it delivered to them, it came to a quite it discovered was that its own internal customers provided many more services and products directly to NASA than it did itself. It became apparent that the overall performance of the parent company in relation to NASA depended a lot more on NASA's perceptions of this team's internal customers than it did on NASA's perceptions of the team.

What Is the Measured Quality of Our Products and Services?

Customer satisfaction is, first of all, a function of the *measured* quality of the product and service that we deliver. Output and customer satisfaction are linked inextricably. Customer satisfaction is, however, more than a function of output. It also is a function of the *perceptions* of customers and the *expectations* of customers. Figure 5-1 suggests how these three variables are related.

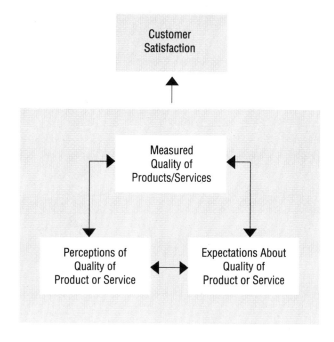

Figure 5-1. Key Variables In Customer Satisfaction

All three variables must be understood and measured when a team is designing projects to improve customer satisfaction. First, let us discuss measurement of the quality of output.

Teams must take four steps to understand the measured quality of their output:

1. Identify the output;
2. Establish the relative importance of the output;
3. Develop measures for assessing the quality of the output; and
4. Use the measures to track and monitor improvement in the quality of the output.

The first three of these steps can be implemented by using a structured process that has proven useful with many teams with which I have worked.

Structured Process To Develop Measured Quality of Output

The sequence in the process is as follows:

1. **Develop clarity about the meaning of output.** Outputs are all the services and products that the team delivers for the use of an internal or external customer. It is useful for a team to refer to its list of customers and to think about each of these customers as it produces its list of outputs. All information that is developed by the team or that the team is expected to use should be recorded and displayed on charts.

2. **Develop clarity about measures of output as *ratios*,** (one thing is compared to another, i.e., production unit to production time or service unit to errors). There are two kinds of measures that teams should start using right away to track the quality of their output. These are measures of *cost* and measures of *attributes*. They are described later in this section.

3. **Develop, by brainstorming, a list of as many outputs as possible.** The sequence for doing this is for the team to peruse its lists of customers and, for each customer, to develop two lists of output, one for *services* and one for *products.*

4. **Review all outputs and ensure that they meet the following criteria:** (a) they are phrased in concrete terms so that there is no question about their exact meaning; (b) they represent something for which the team has total or shared responsibility; (c) the team can directly influence some aspect of the output's quality. *Note:* If the team identifies outputs for which it shares direct responsibility with other teams or organizations, these outputs should be set aside at this point; later, measurements and improvement projects should be developed in conjunction with the other teams or organizations.

5. **Develop criteria and select the outputs for which measures first will be developed.** Criteria can be based on the importance of the customer who is using the output, the relative dollar value of the output, the relative visibility of the output, the relative importance of the output to upper management, the relative amount of the output, etc.

6. **Transfer the first output for which measures will be developed to the top of a separate page of chart paper and draw a line under it.** This is the numerator of the measurement ratio that is being developed. Review this numerator again. Ensure that it clearly describes a concrete output for which the team is held responsible.

7. **Establish as a team the specific kind of measure that will be developed.** A full description of the two kinds of measures that I recommend is found below.

8. **Develop, by brainstorming, a list of the sources of data that the team will use to measure the output.** If

the team is developing a cost measure, the sources of data are things such as travel, planning, direct labor, hardware, rework, etc. If it is an attributes measure, it will be types of errors or failures.

Record the list developed in this step under the numerator (i.e., the output) to be measured. This provides the team with a picture of the relationships that it is trying to establish in the ratios that it is building.

9. **Select from the data sources listed in the denominator the ones that will be tracked.** To select a set of data sources, the team first should establish selection criteria, e.g., availability of data, time spent in acquiring data, amount of information that the data will provide for potential improvement, etc.

10. **Review the ratio and refine it if necessary.**

Defining Output

Outputs can be classified in a number of ways, e.g., resources, equipment, materials, information, services, products. We will use two categories to illustrate the process of designing improvement projects. These are the services and products that a team delivers to internal or external customers. General examples of *services* are:

- technical advice,
- delivery of goods,
- repair of equipment,
- training programs,
- physical examinations,
- arbitration of grievances,
- contact of job candidates,
- processing of claims,

- investigation of accidents, and
- service calls completed.

General examples of *products* are:

- reports,
- budgets,
- machined parts,
- invoices,
- projects,
- software, and
- drawings.

Defining Measures

Authors and researchers have suggested many different ways in which to measure performance. Also, there are a number of different proposals for combining various discrete measures into matrices and indices (e.g., Sink, 1985; Tuttle & Romanowski, 1985). It is not my purpose to develop a comprehensive set of performance measures. My focus at this point is on output, and output has meaning only when it is related to a customer. It is from the point of view of measuring customer satisfaction that I will describe how teams can easily track the quality of their services and products.

There are two measures of quality that teams will find easy to develop, to use in tracking the quality of their output, and to translate into improvement projects. These are measures of *cost* and measures of *attributes.* Cost measures answer questions such as, "How much direct labor was used?" "How much time did it take?" and "Should we make cost reduction an immediate improvement target?" Attribute measures answer questions such as, "What is the ratio of errors to product or service unit?" "How often are there failures?" and "Do we need to improve some aspects of our services or products?"

Because I have indicated that cost is not the primary concern of customers, it may appear that I am contradicting myself by stating that measuring cost is important and that, in fact, it is tied to quality. The relationship of cost to quality is easiest to see when we look at external customers and a company's natural concern for profit. The traditional formula for profit has been:

Selling price = Cost to deliver quality + Profit.

The emphasis here is to charge the customer a price that is computed *after* the amount of profit desired is added to the cost to deliver the service or product. The selling price to the customer is the last consideration. Desired profit margin and cost to deliver are computed first. This formula may work well in environments that are free from competition. It is a formula for certain demise in environments in which our competitors are thinking first of the customer. This formula does not encourage a company to deliver quality and, at the same time, drive down the cost to deliver.

The profit formula that puts the customer first and stimulates continuous improvement is:

Selling price - Profit = Cost to deliver quality.

The emphasis in this formula is to focus first on what the market price for a quality product or service can be and then to achieve profit by relentlessly driving down the costs to deliver that service or product. It is only when every work team reduces the costs of its outputs to its *internal* customers that reduction in the company's costs to deliver its products and services to its *external* customers can be achieved.

The primary way to make a profit in a highly competitive market is to drive down the cost to deliver, not to raise the selling price. When measuring the costs of their services and products, teams are kept focused on driving down every cost related to delivering quality services and products to their internal and external customers.

Knowing what it costs to produce a service or product should lead teams to examine the efficiency and effectiveness of all their work processes. It should make them persistent in eliminating every form of waste and every occurrence of rework.

Measures of Cost. The basic model for this kind of measure is:

$$\frac{\text{Service or product unit}}{\text{Sources of cost}}$$

Note should be made of the way in which the denominator is phrased. Rather than considering "costs," teams should identify as many "*sources* of costs" as possible. By identifying sources of cost, teams will discover costs that they will otherwise overlook, e.g., meetings, informal planning sessions, travel to inspection sites, preplanning time, time spent waiting for decisions, etc.

Examples of measures of costs are:

$$\frac{\text{Number of software changes issued}}{\text{Cost of project-planning meetings, writing code, debugging}}$$

$$\frac{\text{Total number of wind-tunnel tests run}}{\text{Cost of facilities management}}$$

$$\frac{\text{Design reviews}}{\text{Cost of professional staff hours}}$$

$$\frac{\text{Number of quality inspections}}{\text{Cost of planning, travel, reporting}}$$

$$\frac{\text{Number of claims completed}}{\text{Time to complete}}$$

Measures of Attributes. The basic model for this measure is:

$$\frac{\text{Indicators of error, loss, or failure}}{\text{Service or product unit measured}}$$

Measures of attributes compare an output with data about error, loss, or failure. Examples of attribute measures are:

$$\frac{\text{Mistakes in work packages issued}}{\text{Work packages issued}}$$

$$\frac{\text{Unplanned down time of facility}}{\text{Number of tests}}$$

$$\frac{\text{Errors determined by followup}}{\text{Number of safety-inspection reports}}$$

$$\frac{\text{Customer complaints}}{\text{Hours of service}}$$

$$\frac{\text{Modifications required}}{\text{Drawings delivered}}$$

Some time ago, I worked with the Data Processing and Integration Branch at Kennedy Space Center to design some attribute measures. This branch develops software and hardware changes in the Real Time Data System, which supports launches of the Centaur rocket. The Branch makes modifications to the system based on the requests of its internal customers. After these changes are delivered, the branch receives Malfunction Information Reports (MIRs) from customers when any sort of malfunction results from the changes to the Real Time Data System. Using the measurement model for attributes, the branch designed a particularly powerful measurement. The measure derived was:

$$\frac{\text{Sum of weighted MIRs}}{\text{Scheduled system-operation hours}}$$

MIRs were weighted by the following formula:
1 = Unit inoperative
5 = System partially degraded

10 = System seriously degraded
20 = System totally inoperative.

If it is to understand the problems and opportunities related to customer satisfaction, a team first must know the measured quality of its output. Teams also must understand their customers' perceptions and expectations.

Customer Perceptions and Expectations

The role that perceptions and expectations play in customer satisfaction is obvious in service industries (Boothe, 1990). Take the case of the hamburger delivered at a fast-food restaurant. It is not just the quality of the hamburger that is important; it is also the *perceptions* that customers have of how the hamburger is delivered that are important. Furthermore, the satisfaction of customers with their hamburgers also is a matter of how they *expect* the hamburger to appear, taste, and be delivered.

Customer satisfaction is first a function of the measured quality of the hamburger. Measured quality in this case includes the hamburger, the time it takes to deliver the hamburger, the appearance of the hamburger, and the cleanliness and attractiveness of the environment in which the hamburger is delivered. But quality and, ultimately, customer satisfaction also are functions of what the customer perceives about these and other variables.

Customer satisfaction also is a function of expectations. Customers have expectations about their hamburgers. How quickly do customers expect to be served? What do they expect to pay? How do they expect to be treated? What do they expect their hamburgers to look like? These expectations may or may not coincide with the restaurant's understanding of the expectations.

Employee-assistance programs provide short-term personal assistance to employees and serve as central contact points to refer employees to additional sources of help—usually counselors. One employee-assistance team had committed to ensuring that every employee who requested help had an appointment with a counselor within forty-eight hours after making contact with the team. I helped this team to conduct a survey to determine (among other things) the expectations of employees about how soon they expected to be seen by a counselor after they had first contacted the employee-assistance team. More than 90 percent of employees expected to be seen no sooner than three days after initial contact. More than 75 percent of these expected to be seen within a week.

The point of this example is not to demonstrate that the team was committed to providing its customers a service that the customers did not want. The point is that the team did not know what its customers' expectations were. Perceptions and expectations can be determined only through regular, effective contact and feedback.

To understand problems and opportunities related to customer satisfaction, teams must recognize that "no news" from customers (internal or external) is not necessarily "good news." To improve customer satisfaction, teams must make it their jobs to *find out the news* and not wait *to be found out by the news*.

Morrison, Incorporated, is a $689 million, 225-unit restaurant chain that is headquartered in Mobile, Alabama. All customers are invited to call a toll-free number to let Mr. Sandy Beall, the president of Morrison, know how they liked or disliked their dining experiences. Each morning at eight o'clock, Mr. Beall reviews the messages from the previous day and responds to each person who has left a message.

First Chicago Bank is another example. It regularly invites its customers and suppliers to participate in open forums for which the only agenda are the perceptions that people have of the bank.

Personal Contact with Customers

Perceptions and expectations must first of all be monitored by means of personal contact with customers. One of the consistent results of my seminars on total quality and continuous improvement is that teams recognize how little personal contact all the team members have with all their customers. This lack of contact often occurs because teams have not recognized that they have customers, especially internal ones. It also occurs because teams have not made customer contact a norm and have not established it as a clear expectation for team members. For example, the expectation of regular personal contact with internal customers is not made part of job descriptions and hiring interviews.

Lack of personal contact also results from too much structure and hierarchy in the organization. In many organizations, contacts with customers, like decisions, are concentrated disproportionately at the top. It is difficult to develop the habit of customer contact in organizations that are highly stratified, in which organizational boundaries are not highly porous, and in which people feel limited and constricted by their particular jobs.

Take the example of an engineering design group in which only the lead engineer of a project is permitted to talk to the customer who requested the design. First-hand information about customer expectations and perceptions is not available to the people who do the work (draftspersons and other engineers on the project). All such information is filtered, intermittently, through the lead engineer.

No team is without customers, and every member of the team must have regular, personal contact with the team's customers in order to monitor perceptions and expectations. Perceptions and expectations are too changeable and fragile to be monitored intermittently and by a select few.

Personal contact is an absolute requirement for monitoring the perceptions and expectations of customers. It also is necessary to employ more structured or formal methods.

Customer-Satisfier Matrix

The Customer-Satisfier Matrix (Figure 5-2) is a way to measure customer satisfaction that I have used with teams in many different organizations. The actual matrix is developed by the team with the full involvement and collaboration of its customers. Following are the steps for developing the matrix and one example.

Step #1. Decide whether the team is going to identify satisfiers for internal customers or for external ones.

Step #2. Use brainstorming or the nominal group technique to identify all these customers.

Step #3. Select the customer for whom the team will develop a list of satisfiers. The team may choose to use a weighted voting method such as that used with the nominal group technique.

Step #4. Use the brainstorming technique to create a list of possible satisfiers for the customer who was identified in Step 3.

Step #5. Rank the satisfiers according to their relative importance. The team may find it necessary to use a weighted voting method. Select the top five satisfiers.

Step #6. Use the Customer-Satisfier Matrix (Figure 5-2, page 120). List the five satisfiers in the left column. Distribute ten points over the five satisfiers. Assign at least one point to the least important satisfier. Assign no more than five points to the most important satisfier. In column 2, list the assigned weight of importance for each satisfier.

Step #7. In column 3, enter the rating for each satisfier. Use a rating scale of one-to-five for each of the satisfiers. These ratings represent the customer's evaluation of the quality of the team's services or products. The meanings of the numbers in the scale are as follows:

- Rating of 5: No measured or perceived errors, discrepancies, or failures in quality. All services and products delivered are fit to use 100 percent of the time. Customer is extremely positive about team's performance.

- Rating of 4: Only minor errors, discrepancies, or failures in quality. No discrepancies have negative impact on the customer's performance. All services and products still delivered fit to use 100 percent of the time after occasional, minor adjustments.

Team rated: For period from: to:

Customer: Date:

SATISFIERS	WEIGHT	RATING	WT. X RATING	WEIGHTED RATING
1.				
2.				
3.				
4.				
5.				
		SUMMARY RATING		

The highest rating for this measurement matrix is 50. The lowest possible rating is 10.

Figure 5-2. Customer-Satisfier Matrix

- Rating of 3: A few significant errors, discrepancies, or failures in quality are noted. Some services or products require significant attention to be 100 percent fit for use. Possible negative impact on customer's performance.

- Rating of 2: Major errors, discrepancies, or failures in quality are noted. Many services or products require significant attention to be 100 percent fit for use. Some products or services cannot be made fit to use. Clear negative impact on customer's performance. Customer's patience almost exhausted.

- Rating of 1: Errors, discrepancies, or failures in quality are so extensive that most products or services require attention to be fit to use. Many products or services cannot be made fit to use. Major negative impact on customer's performance. Customer's patience exhausted.

Step #8. Enter the weight and multiplier for each satisfier in column 4. Multiply the weight for each satisfier times its rating and enter the result in column 5.

Step #9. List the weighted rating for each satisfier in column 5. Enter the total at the bottom of the column where it says "Summary Rating."

Figure 5-3 is an example of a Customer-Satisfier Matrix developed for a print shop for one of its internal customers.

Team rated: *Printing*   For period of: *1/1/92*   to: *4/1/92*
Customer: *Work Documentation and Control*   Date: *4/12/92*

SATISFIERS	WEIGHT	RATING	WT. X RATING	WEIGHTED RATING
1. Orders on time	3	3.0	3 x 3.0	9.00
2. No content errors	2	4.5	2 x 4.5	9.00
3. Response to changes	2	3.5	2 x 3.5	7.00
4. Technical advice	2	4.0	2 x 4.0	8.00
5. Appearance	1	3.5	1 x 3.5	3.50
			SUMMARY RATING	36.50

The highest rating for this measurement grid is 50. The lowest possible rating is 10.

Figure 5-3. Example: Customer-Satisfier Matrix for Print Shop

The Customer-Satisfier Matrix is a form of survey (see Chapter 2). Additional examples of customer surveys are found in the Appendix.

In this section, I have discussed the first step in designing projects to improve output and customer satisfaction: Understand the opportunity or problem. To achieve such understanding, teams must answer the following questions:

- Who are our customers?
- What is the measured quality of our services and products?
- What are our customers' perceptions of our output, i.e., our services and products?
- What are our customers' expectations of our output?

I also have stated that customer satisfaction is a function of three variables:

- measured quality of services and products,
- perceptions of the quality of services and products, and
- expectations about services and products.

The next step in designing a project to improve output and customer satisfaction is to define the specific improvement target.

STEP 2: DEFINE THE SPECIFIC IMPROVEMENT TARGET

Targets to improve output and customer satisfaction can be derived from specific and immediate problems (e.g., customer complaints), various data sources that measure the costs or attributes of output, feedback from personal contacts, and surveys of the perceptions and expectations of customers. To illustrate this step and the subsequent ones in designing projects to improve output and customer satisfaction, I will use the example from Figure 5-3, Customer-Satisfier Matrix for Print Shop.

An examination of the matrix in the figure indicates that the print shop received an overall rating of 36.50 out of a possible rating of 50.00. Thus, the team has been rated at 73 percent (36.50/50.00 x 100).

The most obvious opportunity for improvement is in the delivery of orders on time. The team already was tracking the "timeliness" attribute of its products with two measures:

$$\frac{\text{Priority-one orders requested}}{\text{Number delivered on time}}$$

$$\frac{\text{Routine orders requested}}{\text{Number delivered on time}}$$

The data from these two measures were analyzed, and the team determined that: (a) 98.7 percent of its priority orders were completed on time, and 87 percent were completed ahead of time; and (b) 97.5 percent of all routine orders were completed on time, and 65 percent were completed ahead of time. The team decided that it needed more information before it could select its specific improvement strategies. It needed to know: (a) whether the customer was reacting more to a failure to deliver priority-one orders on time or more to a failure to deliver routine orders on time; (b) whether the customer was aware of the percentage of times that orders were completed ahead of schedule and, if so, whether it mattered to the customer that orders were finished early; (c) what kinds of orders (e.g., two color, multicolor, stitched, spiral bound, oversize, etc.) were more likely to be late than others; and (d) whether there was any significant delay from the time that an order was completed to the time that it was delivered.

In order to answer its additional questions, the team collected data by means of interviews with its customers, tracking completion times of different kinds of orders (e.g., two color, multicolor, etc.), and analyzing the time that elapsed from completion to delivery of an order.

The team discovered the following:

- Of all orders that were not completed on time, 85 percent were ones that required special art work that was subcontracted out;

- Of all orders that were not completed on time, 15 percent were ones that required modifications and rework because the customer was dissatisfied with the order when it was delivered (i.e., the customer's expectations were different from those of the print shop);

- Some part of the customer's dissatisfaction was caused by the print shop's not keeping the customer regularly advised about the progress of an order and whether any problems were developing;
- The average time between completion and delivery of both priority-one and routine orders was thirteen hours.

The team decided on the following specific improvement projects:

1. Reduce delay caused by suppliers of art work.
2. Reduce rework caused by lack of clarity about customer's expectations.
3. Improve customer's awareness about progress of order and special problems.
4. Reduce time between completion and delivery of priority-one orders by 50 percent.
5. Reduce time between completion and delivery of routine orders by 50 percent.

STEP 3: DESIGN STRATEGIES TO REACH THE TARGET

I will use the print shop's first two improvement targets to illustrate the design of strategies. The team used the nominal group technique and selected the following strategies.

To reduce the delay caused by its suppliers of art work, it determined to do the following:

1. Develop with its suppliers of art work a set of performance and evaluation criteria that would be used to select and evaluate supplier performance.
2. Monitor suppliers' performance weekly. Give feedback to suppliers and designate improvement targets as appropriate.

To reduce the delay caused by rework, the team decided on an experiment. It would:

1. Form a select team of intake clerks and shop people to design a new order form.

2. Use the form on an experimental basis and compare results (amount of rework) with results from using the current order form.

3. Evaluate the experiment and adjust strategy as needed.

STEP 4: DESIGN THE DATA LINKS

The fourth step in project design is to design the data links to track performance and to anticipate necessary adjustments. Data links are designed at various times in an improvement project. Sometimes the data links that we design to understand a problem are the ones that we use to track the progress of a project. If, in the case of the print shop, the team undertakes its various projects to improve customer satisfaction with the shop's performance in delivering "orders on time," the Customer-Satisfier Matrix becomes a data link for monitoring the team's progress. To further illustrate the design of data links, let us use the targets and strategies described in Steps 2 and 3 above.

The strategy that the team selected to improve its suppliers' performance was to develop a set of performance criteria. It designed its measurement links with these criteria. It monitored performance against these criteria by recording for each product received whether it was on time, early, or late, and whether it met expectations. It further monitored how well each supplier kept the shop informed about problems and delays.

To reduce the delay caused by rework, the team decided to test a new order form. Data links were designed to compare performance on orders taken with the test form and performance on orders taken with the old form.

STEP 5: DESIGN THE RESPONSE PROCESS TO USE DATA FROM THE DATA LINKS

Intake-order clerks were made responsible for retrieving the data about the results of the old and the experimental order forms. They also were made responsible for reporting the data (in the form agreed) to the project team on Wednesday and Friday of each week. The project team assumed responsibility for responding to the data.

STEP 6: DETERMINE HOW THE PROJECT WILL BE MANAGED

The design for managing the project included the following:

- **Overall Responsibility.** A mechanic from the first shift was assigned responsibility for the project and its five specific objectives. The project team was composed of the mechanic, the intake-order clerks, and the members of the special team that designed the experimental order form.

- **Milestones.** Some of the milestones that the team adopted were: date on which performance criteria would be completed for suppliers; date to start collecting data on supplier performance; date on which such data first would be reported; and period of time for the experiment using the new order form.

- **Progress of the Project.** This was reported weekly at the team's regular TQM meeting.

- **Resources.** The mechanic responsible for the project kept an account of time spent on the project and reported to the whole team (entire print shop) any problem with time or other resources.

- **Records.** Records to be kept included data from run charts and bar charts, minutes from discussions of the project at TQM meetings, and a summary of the project when it ended.

SUMMARY

In this chapter, I have described how to design projects to improve customer satisfaction. I have suggested that:

1. There are differences between internal and external customers that must be taken into account.
2. Customer satisfaction has less to do with price than it has to do with:

   • quality of product,
   • quality of service, and
   • quality of treatment.

3. Output (services and products) only has meaning as it is related to customer satisfaction, but this satisfaction is a function of more than output. It also is a function of the *perceptions* of customers and the *expectations* of customers.

I have described the six steps in designing projects to improve output and customer satisfaction and have introduced a variety of specific tools and techniques that can be used with these steps.

In the next chapter, we will look at work processes and how they can be targeted for improvement projects.

Chapter 6

Improving and Measuring
Work Processes

There are four general areas in which teams have the opportunity and obligation to develop projects for continuous improvement: team development, output and customer satisfaction, work processes, and input and supplier performance. The topic of this chapter is the third area, work processes.

DEFINITION OF A WORK PROCESS

A process is a sequence of steps by which work or a task is accomplished. All work is accomplished through one or more processes. Processes exist in every enterprise and business. All products are manufactured by means of processes. All services are delivered by means of processes.

A work *process* is the movement or *flow* of an *object* (part, piece of paper, etc.) through a sequence of *steps* from the point of *input* to the point of *output* (see Figure 2-3). In production processes, this flow typically includes the elements of *transport, delay, operations,* and *inspection.*

The *object* is whatever moves through the steps and is acted on or changed in some way. The object may be a report, an idea, metal stock, a car frame, a plan, a computer chip, an invoice, or anything else that must be moved or modified in order to prepare it for output to some other process or for delivery to an internal or external customer.

Transport refers to the movement of the object in the flow from one step to the next step. An example of transport in a manufacturing process is the movement of stock for a crankshaft to a cutting lathe and then its movement from the lathe to the next step or operation in the process. An example of transport in an administrative process is the movement of a travel request from the desk of the clerk who prepared it to the supervisor who must sign it. Transport also includes the communication of information or ideas from one person to another or from one operation to another.

Delay refers to the time in which the object is waiting in its flow through the process. For example, delay occurs when materials are delivered and await the beginning of a manufacturing process or the time when a travel request sits on a supervisor's desk. Delay occurs in most administrative processes when decisions are required, when additional information must be added, and when signatures must be obtained. All materials in inventory represent delay.

Operations are the actions that are taken to transform an object from a less desirable to a more desirable state, e.g., a welder transforms two plates in a ship's hull into a single plate; an accountant transforms tax data into a return; a draftsperson turns engineers' specifications into finished drawings; a researcher transforms data into conclusions and predictions. An operation can occur at any place in a process. The first operation in responding to a mail order for a product might be to sort the mail. The last operation might be to post the packaged product to the customer.

What we choose to consider a process at any given time is, to some degree, arbitrary. We may consider the entire set of steps in the flow of procurement—from request to delivery of goods—as a single process. Or we may divide this large process into two processes that are joined together so that the output from the first process becomes the input for the second process. We may place the steps of initiating, preparing, approving, and forwarding a purchase request into the first process and put receiving, inspecting, and delivering into the second process. Or we may choose to break each of these two larger processes into the smaller processes of initiating, preparing, approving, forwarding, receiving, etc.

The limits or dimensions of a process are defined by input and output (Figure 2-3). Whenever we can identify an input, we can consider that as the beginning of a process. Whenever we can identify an output, we can consider that as the end of a process.

Some processes consist of steps and operations that are largely under the control of a single individual. These include writing a report; preparing an order release; welding component parts of an automobile frame; conducting a facilities safety inspection; delivering internal mail; and ordering supplies.

Processes more often consist of steps that involve a number of people. Such processes include carrying out a maintenance work order; hauling a boat; preparing travel documents; preparing and delivering paychecks; paying supplier accounts; cutting and milling; and preparing an engineering design.

WAYS TO IMPROVE A PROCESS

Figure 1-1 indicates that there are five main strategies for undertaking improvement projects. The five strategies exist along a continuum from reactive to proactive. Responding primarily is a reactive strategy; creating primarily is a proactive strategy. When we apply these labels to the improvement of work processes, our projects can be cataloged as ones of:

- **Responding** to problems as they occur and fixing what malfunctions or breaks, e.g., data lost, machine out of alignment, error in a report, failure to inspect;

- **Preventing** the occurrence or recurrence of a problem by anticipating an event or by putting safeguards in place, e.g., instituting new maintenance procedures, increasing the number of quality checks, improving the skills of operators, requiring new or more reports;

- **Upgrading** some aspect of a process, e.g., computerizing a step or operation, streamlining a report form, replacing a machine with a new model;

- **Experimenting** by changing some aspect of a process and testing the results, e.g., testing a new tool or machine, testing a new piece of software, changing a sequence; and

- **Creating** a new process to replace an old one, e.g., radically changing a sequence of steps or operations, computerizing a process that was done manually.

There are three types of improvement goals that can be pursued or results that can be achieved in projects to improve work processes. Teams can:

- **Make the process stable:** Ensure that the distribution of the measures taken by the team to determine the performance of the process falls within limits or ranges that should be expected.

- **Reduce the variation in the process:** Improve the process so that the distribution of the measures the team takes to determine the performance of the process comes closer and closer together and, therefore, becomes closer to the average of the measure.

- **Improve the average:** Move the total process to a higher level of performance so that the average of the measures that the team takes to determine the performance of the process becomes significantly higher or lower (depending on the desired direction).

Figure 6-1 shows how these improvement results are related to the five strategies for improvement. The figure conveys the following points:

1. Substantial and long-term improvement takes place in a work process only when we make the process more stable, reduce its variation, or improve its average. The more proactive our improvement strategies are, the more

likely it is that we will make a substantial and long-term improvement.

2. The strategy of responding to problems and fixing what breaks will improve the process (in the sense of keeping it going) but this strategy will never make the process more stable, reduce its variation, or improve its average performance.

3. Preventing an occurrence or recurrence of a problem will improve the stability of the process and reduce its variation but this strategy, alone, is not likely to improve the average performance of the process, i.e., move it to a higher level.

Improvement Strategies	Results		
	Make Stable	Reduce Variation	Improve Average
1. Responding			
2. Preventing	x	x	
3. Upgrading	x	x	x
4. Experimenting	x	x	x
5. Creating	x	x	x

Figure 6-1. Strategies and Results in Work-Process Improvement

4. The strategies of upgrading, experimenting, and creating can improve the stability of a process, reduce its variation, and move it to a higher level of performance.[1]

---

[1] Responding to problems, alone (fixing what breaks), will not make processes stable, reduce variation, or improve the average performance of a process. Preventing problems can stabilize a process and reduce certain kinds of variation. But preventing problems will not, itself, improve the average performance or process.

Teams must understand the meanings of terms such as distribution, average, variation, and stability if they are to engage systematically in the continuous improvement and measurement of their work processes. Definitions of these terms follow, and additional information is provided in the Appendix.

DISTRIBUTION

When we measure something—such as the number of errors per purchasing order—over a period of time, it is likely that the recorded measurements will not all be the same. The measures will make up a distribution. A distribution is a set of measurements of something. When we make a graph or chart of our measurements, we can see what the distribution looks like. Histograms, run charts, and control charts (discussed in Chapter 2) are ways to display graphically or chart a distribution.

AVERAGE

The three most common ways to measure the center of a distribution are the average, the median, and the mode. The only one that will concern us in this book is the average. The usual formula for computing an average is:

$$\overline{X} \ \frac{X_1 + X_2...X_n}{n}$$

Where: $X_{1...n}$ are the measurements taken, and
n = the sample size or total number of measures.

Suppose that Figure 6-2 represents a record, made over a period of three months, of the gas mileage of the family car. The average, X, for the first sample or subgroup is:

$$\frac{21.4 + 19.4 + 18.4 + 19.3 + 18.5}{5}$$

= 19.4.

DATA-COLLECTION SHEET										
Target: Family Car				Measure: mpg			Date(s): 4-7/92			
Date										
Sample	1	2	3	4	5	6	7	8	9	10
	21.4	21.6	22.5	23.4	21.7	18.3	17.9	19.7	17.9	18.4
	19.4	17.7	19.5	19.4	20.2	20.6	19.2	18.5	20.3	15.6
	18.4	18.7	20.4	23.6	24.6	20.3	20.8	17.4	19.5	17.1
	19.3	21.3	22.5	22.9	21.1	19.8	18.1	18.2	19.1	16.4
	18.5	19.5	21.4	20.8	21.5	20.6	19.6	17.1	18.4	15.9
$\overline{X}$	19.4	19.8	21.3	22.0	21.8	19.9	19.1	18.2	19.0	16.8
$\overline{\overline{X}}$: 19.7	Notes: S($\overline{X}$) = 1.63									

Figure 6-2. Gas Mileage for Family Car

When we use the average to establish the center of a process, we actually are using an average of the averages of a number of sets of measurements or separate samples. Our process average is:

$$\frac{19.4 + 19.8 + 21.3 + 22.0 + 21.8 + 19.9 + 19.1 + 18.2 + 19.0 + 16.8}{10}$$

$$= 19.7.$$

VARIATION

Variation is the amount of spread in a distribution, i.e., how far away from the center or average our measures are. Figure 6-3 shows graphs of three distributions. In graph A, some measures are far away from the center, i.e., there is a lot of spread or variation. In graph B, most of the measures are close to the center, so there is less variation than is found in graph A. Graph C represents the *normal* distribution, which is the foundation for most control charts.

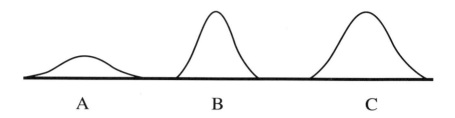

A   B   C

Figure 6-3. Variation

Two Kinds of Variation

The purpose of measuring a process is to learn how the process is performing in regard to the quality that we are measuring. This means that we select a significant aspect of the process, which becomes our "quality indicator" and measure that aspect over time. We also will want to know how our measurements vary in relation to the average.

We can learn two things by measuring variation. First, we can learn how much difference, or "spread," there is among the measurements of our quality indicator. If, for example, the quality indicator that we are measuring is the time it takes to settle accident claims, we can learn just how close the average of our samples is to the overall average time for settling claims. Second, we can learn if the variation in the process is stable. If the process is stable, the great majority of variation among measures that we observe is attributed to chance or *general causes.*

General Causes

General causes are purely chance happenings. They are part of the process in that they result from causes that are common to the process, but none of these causes are predictable. They may not ployees, slight variations in the speed of data entry, and lesser or greater degrees of cooperation by clients.

Special Causes

If the process is not stable, some variation among our measures is attributable to *special causes*. Such causes are not random, and there is a greater difference among measures than would be expected if chance alone were the operative effect. In the case of the accident claims, these causes might be things such as a computer going down, a key employee leaving, a new legal requirement, or a departmental reorganization.

If a work process is stable, to improve its performance we must do something that changes the amount of *all* the variation in the process. For example, if the processing of claims is found to be stable, to improve the system we must do something that reduces the time it takes to complete every claim.

If, however, we find that the process is not stable, we must take two steps to improve the process. First, we must *eliminate the special causes of variation,* e.g., make up the skill deficit caused by losing a key employee or increase the reliability of a computer. Once we have removed the special causes of variation, the process will become stable. Then, if we are to *improve the performance of the process,* we must find a way to reduce the time taken to process all claims all the time.

How To Measure Variation

The typical way to measure the center of a distribution is to compute the average. The most common way to measure the variation in a distribution is to compute the *range* or *standard deviation.*

Range is a statistic that measures the distance between the two most extreme measures in a distribution, the smallest and the greatest. The formula for computing a range is:

$$R = X_2 - X_1$$

Where: X_2 = the greatest measure, and X_1 = the smallest measure.

The standard deviation is a statistic that estimates the total amount of variation there is around the average of a sample distribution. The formula for computing a standard deviation is:

$$s = \sqrt{\frac{\Sigma(x_i - \overline{X})^2}{(n-1)}}$$

Where:
x = each individual measure,
$\overline{X}$ = the average of the measures,
n = the total number of measures, and
Σ = sum of.

The standard deviation computed from the gas-mileage data in Figure 6-2 is 1.63 mpg.[2]

STABILITY

A process is stable if the distribution of the measurements we take of a quality indicator is predictable in relation to the average (center) and spread (variation) of the distribution. Figure 6-4 shows the behavior of three distributions over time.

In example A, the variation or spread of the distribution is stable, but the center or average of the distribution is shifting upward. To return again to the example of processing accident claims, example A would indicate that the average time taken to process claims is increasing, but the amount of variation among times is staying the same.

---

[2]The standard deviation is used to compute the upper and lower control limits of control charts. In actual practice, however, these limits are estimated by using tables found in any text on quality control.

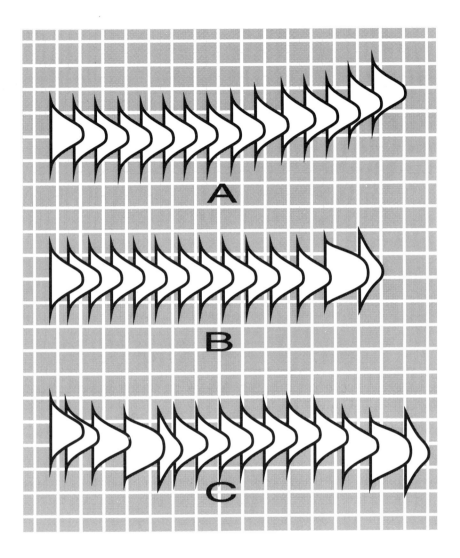

Figure 6-4. Unstable Processes

In example B, the center (average) is stable, but the variation is not. Again, if this is a distribution of our time to process accident claims, our average time is staying the same, but the variation among times is changing.

In example C, both the center and the variation of the distribution are unstable. This distribution suggests that our average time is unpredictable, and the amount of difference among our times in processing claims is unpredictable.

Figure 6-5 is an example of a process whose center and variation are stable.

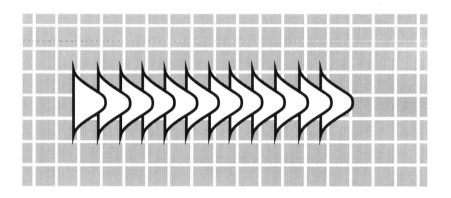

Figure 6-5. Stable Process

Measuring Stability

We can decide whether or not a process is stable by using the concepts of center and variation and by computing the statistics for a distribution of average, range, and standard deviation. A process is stable if the measurements of a set of sample averages for a quality indicator fall within three standard deviations above or below the average of these sample averages. The measurement of three standard deviations above the average is called the upper control limit (UCL) and the measurement of three standard deviations below the average is called the lower control limit (LCL).

The Use and Meaning of Control Limits

Control limits are statistics that tell us what to expect from a process that is performing in a predictable or stable manner. We know that the averages of a series of sample measures will be distributed as in Figure 6-6 (page 142) when the process is stable, i.e., when the variation among these sample averages occurs because of general or chance causes. We can expect that our sample averages will be distributed as follows: 68.26 percent will be within one standard deviation of the average, 95.46 percent will be within two standard deviations of the average, and 99.73 percent will be within three standard deviations of the average. Control limits are computed in various ways, depending on the data that are being used and the type of control chart that is being constructed.

The following section contains an illustration of a control chart. Definitions of the various types of control charts are found in the Appendix, along with information about computing control limits for each type of chart.

Control-Chart Illustration

Control charts use the average performance of a process and the standard deviations of the process to establish control limits. Control limits are not specification limits. Control limits do not describe what we want to get from a process in terms of quality; they describe what we reasonably can expect to get from an existing process.

Figure 6-7 (page 143) shows three examples of an $\overline{X}$ control chart. Example A shows a process that is stable. This process typically is described as "being under statistical control." This simply means that 99.6 percent of our measures fall within plus or minus three standard deviations from the average for the process. The process is predictable. The differences among our measures are attributed to chance causes. If we want to improve the process, we must find ways to reduce the variation among all our measures, i.e., change some step or operation that affects the whole process.

Example B in Figure 6-7 shows a process that is not stable. A number of measures are outside our control limits. We can assume that the causes for these measures are special; they are not general causes and do not result merely from chance. We must remove

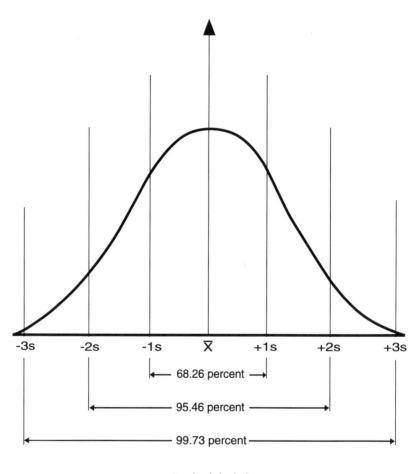

-3s   -2s   -1s $\overline{X}$ +1s   +2s   +3s

68.26 percent

95.46 percent

99.73 percent

s = standard deviation

Figure 6-6. Standard Normal Distribution

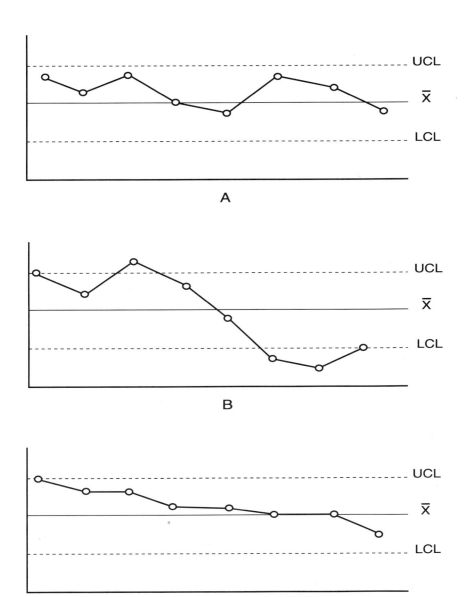

Figure 6-7. Examples of $\overline{X}$ Control Charts

these special causes in order to make the process stable—to bring it under statistical control.

Example C represents a process that has improved over time in such a way that all our measures now are well within the control limits that were computed earlier for the process. It now is time to recompute the system's average and to define new control limits.

The remainder of this chapter is devoted to using all the concepts presented above, along with some of the TQM tools already described, to design process-improvement projects. It will use as an outline the steps of the General Design for Improvement and Measurement Projects presented in Chapter 2.

STEP 1: UNDERSTAND THE OPPORTUNITY OR PROBLEM

There are at least two actions that a team can take to understand a work process: (a) make a flow chart of the process and (b) collect, organize, and analyze data to measure the performance of the process.

Chart the Process

Many work processes have developed over considerable periods of time and have been modified by managers, supervisors, and others of varying degrees of enlightenment. Processes can be influenced by whim and bias. One of the most outstanding characteristics of processes is that they rarely are fully understood.

No one in the organization may know all the steps in a particular process, how necessary each of the steps is, how much time is taken by each step, or how many steps are redundant. Most of the information that people have is based on their own experience of a system or on an outdated description of the system. Every time that I have observed a work team (or ad hoc team) attempt to identify all the steps and operations in a process, I have observed the members' surprise at their own discoveries. They invariably find steps and processes that some of them had no idea existed. They also, invariably, find steps or operations that serve no purpose. *Processes that are not fully understood or that are left alone over time usually will drift toward lower and lower quality.*

Figure 6-8 (page 146) is an example of a flow chart of a process for issuing travel authorizations that a team produced before it attempted to improve the process. Figure 6-9 (page 147) is a flow chart of the improved process after the team had eliminated non-value-added operations and had reduced the number of steps.

Collect, Organize, and Analyze Data To Measure the Performance of the Process

Teams can, of course, improve a process "intuitively" by charting it and eliminating or shortening steps or operations. I have never seen a team examine a flow chart of a process and not perceive opportunities for improvement. However, teams must monitor the performance of a process (by taking measurements over time) if they are truly to improve it. A flow chart of the process should be created every six months or so, and measurement should be done continually.

Histograms and Pareto charts group data and show static displays (snapshots) of the performance of the process. Run charts and control charts show the performance of the process over time (a moving picture of the performance). Run charts and control charts, then, show us trends and patterns.

The team that made the flow chart of the travel-approval process decided to measure the performance of the new process (Figure 6-9). It selected two quality indicators. The first one was the time that the team took to process documents from the point of request to the time that procurement documents were issued. The second quality indicator selected was the total number of errors for all procurement documents prepared for final signature.

To track its first quality indicator, the team took one sample a week of five completed travel documents and recorded the time it

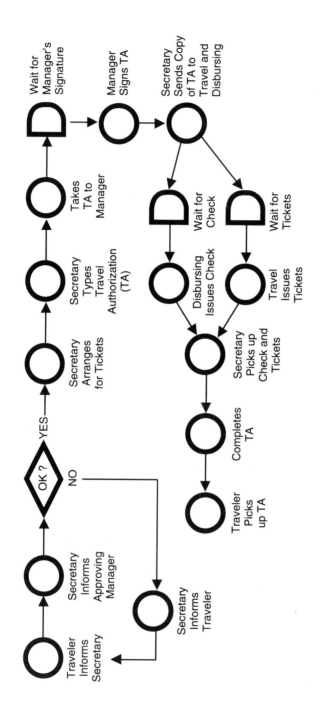

Figure 6-8. Flow Chart of Original Travel-Approval Process

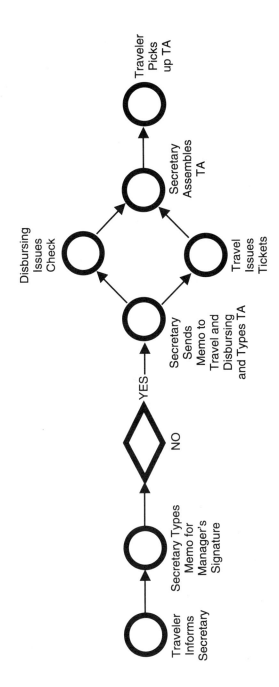

Figure 6-9. Flow Chart of Improved Travel-Approval Process

took to process each document. It computed the average time for each sample for ten weeks. Figure 6-10 is a data-collection sheet for the ten samples. Figure 6-11 is an $\overline{X}R$ control chart that the team made of the process.

DATA-COLLECTION SHEET										
Target: *Procurement Process*				Measure: *Hours*			Date(s): *4/1-6/15*			
Date:	Week									
	1	2	3	4	5	6	7	8	9	10
Sample	11.7	5.2	6.2	6.4	5.0	6.7	6.1	6.8	6.0	6.9
	11.9	6.8	5.6	7.3	6.6	4.7	6.9	5.1	5.5	7.2
	9.6	4.4	5.7	7.5	3.7	7.7	6.9	6.8	4.7	6.8
	10.5	5.6	4.8	6.8	7.9	8.5	6.4	6.2	6.9	4.5
	12.9	4.0	5.6	5.2	4.5	5.5	5.0	4.4	5.0	4.8
$\overline{X}$	11.3	5.2	5.6	6.6	5.5	6.6	6.3	5.9	5.6	6.0
Range	3.3	2.8	1.4	2.3	4.2	3.8	1.9	2.4	2.2	2.7
$\overline{\overline{X}}$: 6.5	$s(\overline{X})$ = 1.76 UCL = 11.78 LCL = 1.22									
$\overline{R}$: 2.7	$s(R)$ = .86 UCL = 5.28 LCL = .12									

Figure 6-10. Data-Collection Sheet for Procurement Process

The conclusions that the team drew from an examination of these control charts were as follows:

1. The process was stable in reference to its average.
2. The process was stable in reference to its range.
3. Both the $\overline{X}R$ charts suggested that the process was moving to higher performance levels and that new control limits should be calculated.

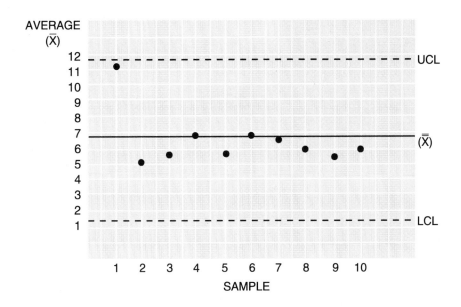

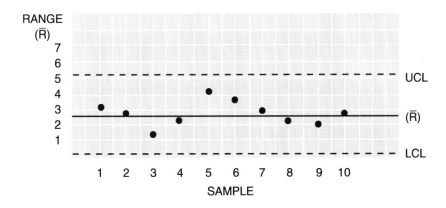

Figure 6-11. $\overline{X}$ R Control Chart of Procurement Process

To track the second indicator (the total number of errors), the team selected fifty sets of documents for eight successive weeks and recorded the total number of errors for each on the data sheet shown in Figure 6-12.

DATA SHEET									
Target: Procurement Documents	Period: *Each week for 8 weeks beginning 4/92*								
	Period								
	1	2	3	4	5	6	7	8	Total
Order Nos.	8	5	3	2	2	2	3	5	30
Request Errors	3	2		4	2	1	1	1	14
Description	3	2	2	2	3	2	1	1	16
Address	2	1	2	3		1	1	1	11
Priority No.		1		2	1	2		1	7
Data Missing	4	3	2	3	3	1	1		17
Misspellings		2	1	3	2	1	1		10
Suspense Dates	1	1	1	3	1	1	1		9
All Others	1		1	1			1	1	5
Total	22	17	12	23	14	11	10	10	119

Figure 6-12. Data Sheet for Procurement Errors

From the data sheet, the team constructed the c control chart shown in Figure 6-13 (page 151). It then constructed the Pareto diagram shown in Figure 6-14 (page 152), in order to display the relative frequency of each kind of error made.

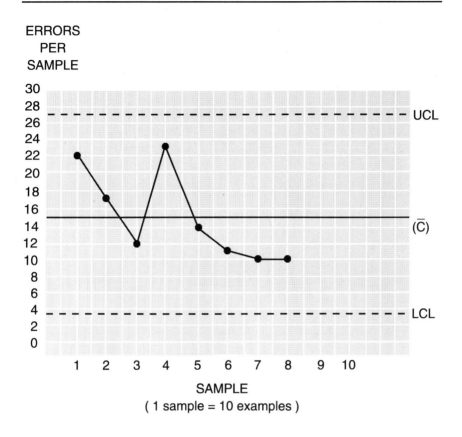

Figure 6-13. C Control Chart of Procurement Processing Errors

$$\overline{C} = \frac{total\ no.\ of\ errors}{no.\ of\ units\ observed} = \frac{119}{8} = 14.88$$

$$UCL = \overline{C} + 3\sqrt{\overline{C}} = 14.88 + 3\ (3.85) = 26.43$$

$$LCL = \overline{C} - 3\sqrt{\overline{C}} = 14.88 - 3\ (3.85) = 3.33$$

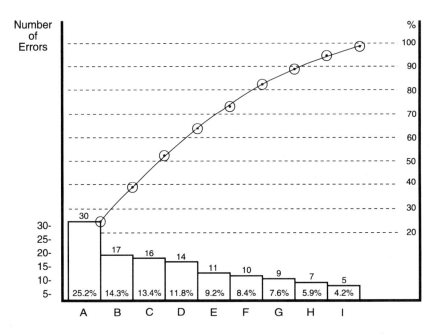

A=Order number error; B=Data missing; C=Description error; D=Request error;
E=Address error; F=Misspelling; G=Wrong suspense date;
H=Wrong priority number; I=All other sources of error

Order number error = 30/119 = 25.2%
Data missing = 17/119 = 14.3%, cum. = 39.3%
Description error = 16/119 = 13.4%, cum. 52.7%
Request error = 14/119 = 11.8%, cum. = 64.5%
Address error = 11/119 = 9.2%, cum. = 73.7%
Misspelling = 10/119 = 8.4%, cum. = 82.1%
Wrong suspense dates = 9/119 = 7.6%, cum. 89.7%
Wrong priority number = 7/119 = 5.9%, cum. = 95.6%
All others = 5/119 = 4.2%, cum. = 99.8%

Figure 6-14.   Pareto Chart of Errors in Procurement Process

The team analyzed the data and came to the following conclusions about the process:

1. It was stable in reference to the total number of errors made per week. No measurements were outside the upper control limit of 26.43 or the lower control limit of 3.33.

2. Total errors from week one and week four were 22 and 23, respectively. These numbers began to approach the upper control limits and required further analysis.

3. Errors in order numbers accounted for 25 percent of all errors, and order-number errors plus data missing and errors in descriptions of procurements accounted for better than half of all errors (52.7 percent).

4. Beginning in the fifth week, there was a decline in total errors, which lasted until the eighth week.

These data pointed toward specific improvement opportunities.

STEP 2: DEFINE THE IMPROVEMENT TARGET

The team concluded that it would work on two improvement opportunities, as follows:

1. Reduce the average time to process procurement requests —from request to final signature—to 4.30 hours, and

2. Reduce errors in order numbers to zero.

STEP 3: DESIGN STRATEGIES TO REACH THE TARGET

The team decided to run two experiments. To reduce total processing time, the team decided to computerize the initial data-entry phase of the process and to test this change with one of its internal customers, the computer services department. The experiment called for the use of existing software and networks so that the customer could make a procurement request and verify the information in the request without the use of paper forms and the physical transmittal of such forms.

The team's strategy to reduce errors in order numbers to zero was to test a new procedure for entering and verifying these numbers. Under this procedure, order numbers were recorded in reverse order and verified as the final step in completing a procurement package. A confirmation signature (by the clerk responsible for the package) also was required. These changes were entered in the processing manual.

STEP 4: DESIGN THE DATA LINKS

The data link to track the experiment to improve total processing time consisted of recording two points in the process: (a) the time automatically recorded by the computer clock when a request was made by the customer and (b) the entry in the existing log of the date and time a procurement package was sent to the mail room.

The data link to track errors in order numbers was the same as was used in Step 1. Errors were counted for ten samples of ten examples taken once a week. The team determined that these data would be recorded on a data sheet (as in Figure 6-12) and that a c-control chart would be drawn as data became available (as in Figure 6-13).

STEP 5: DESIGN THE RESPONSE PROCESS TO USE DATA FROM THE DATA LINKS

The project teams responsible for the two experiments tracked their respective experiments and were required to:

1. Report the results of their experiments at the procurement team's weekly TQM meeting;
2. Recommend, each week, whether the experiments should be continued;
3. Make recommendations about incorporating the experimental changes into the regular procurement process; and
4. Provide plans for making permanent changes in the procurement process based on the results of the experiments.

STEP 6: DETERMINE HOW THE PROJECT WILL BE MANAGED

The design for managing the project included the following:

- **Overall Responsibility.** A separate procurement clerk was given responsibility for each of the two projects. A supervisor and secretary were added to each of the teams. Responsibility for the experiment to input the customer's request electronically was assumed jointly by the project team and one member from the customer's team (the computer services department). Responsibilities and projected start and finish dates were recorded on a Project Management Form.

Improvement target: *Reduce processing time to 4.3 hrs. and errors to 0.* Date Begun: *1/92*			Project lead: *Jill* Date Completed:	
Planned Actions	Start Date	End Date	Responsible	Notes
Develop and test new computer-entry process	1/1	4/1	Jack	Coordinate with all customers
New procedure for entering order nos.	1/1		Kevin	Coordinate with all team members
Weekly sample of processing time	1/1		Jill	Continue unless team decides to stop
Weekly sample of errors	1/1		Kevin	Continue unless team decides to stop
Report progress of project to team	1/15		Jill	Continue to end of project

Figure 6-15. Project Management Form

- **Milestones.** Some of the milestones that the team adopted for the project to test the experimental input system were: date the new process would be ready to test, date on which first data from test would begin, and date for first report to procurement team. Milestones for the experiment to test new procedure for entering and checking order numbers included: date on which the new procedure would be entered in the processing manual, date the new procedure would begin, and date on which first data would be reported to procurement team (Figure 6-16).

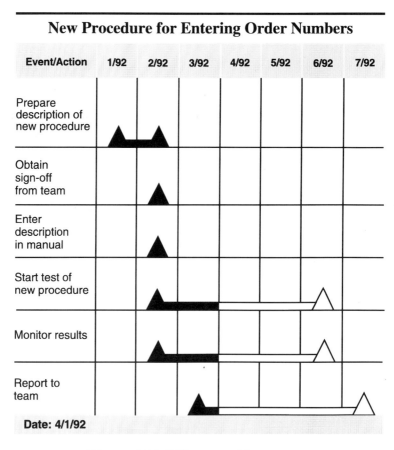

Figure 6-16. Milestones Chart

- **Progress of the Project.** Reported weekly at the team's regular TQM meeting.

- **Resources.** The clerk responsible for each project was required to keep an account of time spent on the project and to report any problem with time or other resources.

- **Records.** Records to be kept included data from data sheets, control charts, and Pareto diagrams; minutes from discussion of the project at TQM team meetings; and a summary of the project when it ended.

SUMMARY

This chapter has presented preliminary concepts that teams must understand in order to design projects to improve their work processes. These concepts are:

1. Definition of a work process;

2. The five general strategies of responding, preventing, upgrading, experimenting, and creating and suggestions about what each of these strategies is capable of achieving;

3. The three ways to improve a process: (a) make the process stable, (b) reduce the variation in the process, and (c) improve the average performance of the process;

4. The meanings of key statistical terms that are part of designing and using control charts (e.g., distribution, average, general variation, special variation, stability, and control limits);

5. How to compute the average, range, and standard deviation for a distribution;

6. How to apply the use of the average and standard deviation when computing control limits;

7. How control limits relate to the normal distribution and how these limits can be used to determine the stability of a process; and

8. Examples of how to use statistical and TQM tools to design process-improvement projects.

The next chapter will address the fourth and final focus for improvement projects: input and supplier performance.

Chapter 7

Improving and Measuring
Input and Supplier Performance

$\mathbf{W}$e now have examined three of the four areas that teams and organizations should target for continuous improvement and measurement (Figure 1-1). They are:

- the context of team development,
- output and customer satisfaction, and
- work processes.

In this chapter, I will discuss the fourth area for improvement: input and supplier performance. There are three considerations that are related to this topic.

First, much of what can be said about improving input and supplier performance can be inferred from what I have already written about output and customer satisfaction. Also, because teams occupy—at various times—all three key roles (processor, customer, and supplier) in the performance or production system, they easily can use their experience as suppliers to understand how to improve the performance of their own suppliers, just as they can use their experience as customers to improve the satisfaction of their own customers.

Second, this book focuses on teams and what they can do to undertake continuous improvement. Although I have used examples concerning total organizations to illustrate points, the purpose of this book is to provide teams with help in designing improvement projects; it is not concerned with the larger organizational issues of strategic planning and total-quality initiatives. In discussing supplier performance, therefore, I will focus on what a team (of whatever kind and position in an organization) can do to improve, at its level, the performance of its suppliers. I will not discuss in any detail organizational issues that relate to large-scale purchases, sole-source suppliers, supplier surveillance, legal aspects of supplier relations, supplier-qualification processes, and the like.

A third consideration is that the nature of the service or product that is required will influence the relationship that a customer must establish with a supplier and will, subsequently, influence how the customer assesses the supplier's performance. Supplier and customer may have at least the number of different relationships described below:

1. The customer knows exactly what it wants. The product or service is available at the same quality from more than one supplier. The only determining criterion for selection is price.

2. The variables in this relationship are the same, except that there is a difference in the quality of the service or product that is available, and price no longer is the only criterion.

3. The customer requires the assistance of its suppliers in order to identify its needs. Selection criteria include the capability of the supplier to deliver technical assistance to determine these needs (e.g., by submitting a design, identifying alternative system components, helping the customer to clarify its specifications, modifying the customer's initial specifications, etc.).

Every work team depends on internal and external suppliers. These suppliers may be at a peer level or represent a subset of a larger supplier organization. For example, EG&G Florida has a large base-support contract at NASA's Kennedy Space Center. The primary character of NASA's relationship with EG&G is not defined at just the executive level or across a single interface. Customer and supplier relations exist over hundreds of interfaces between the various EG&G Florida working units and their NASA counterparts, e.g., between design-engineering teams, between quality-assurance teams, between computer-services teams, etc.

The term "supplier" here means the individuals and groups on which some specific organizational unit or team depends directly and with whom it has direct contact.

Before addressing the topic of designing projects for improving and measuring the input and performance of suppliers with whom the team regularly interacts and on whom it routinely depends, we need to clarify the following preliminary topics:

- The relationships of the other improvement areas to supplier performance;
- The differences between external and internal suppliers; and
- How to make suppliers members of the team.

THE RELATIONSHIP OF SUPPLIER PERFORMANCE TO THE OTHER AREAS OF IMPROVEMENT

The Model for Continuous Improvement and Measurement (Figure 2-1) is intended to communicate the following about improvement and measurement:

1. The final goal toward which all improvement is directed is output and customer satisfaction. The success and survival of teams and total organizations depends on their ability to accept their internal and external customers as the final arbiters of quality and the ultimate judges of their continued existence.

2. Team development provides the potential for improvement and the context within which all other improvement strategies and actions should be designed. Any action or strategy that is not fully compatible with team development

ultimately will prove dysfunctional to the larger plan for continuous improvement.

The application of team development to continuous improvement provides these specific guidelines for continuous improvement:

1. Teams are the primary units of productivity and must be the focus for continuous improvement.

2. Teams can best equip themselves for continuous improvement by first addressing their own development.

3. The general strategy for improving customer satisfaction is to make the team's customers part of the team.

4. The general strategy for improving work processes is through team action.

5. The general strategy for improving input and supplier performance is to make the team's suppliers part of the team.

DIFFERENCES BETWEEN EXTERNAL AND INTERNAL SUPPLIERS

A supplier is any person or group on which the team depends for input of anything that it must use to produce its own output and to satisfy its own customers. Inputs include resources, materials, equipment, information, services, and products. As I did in the discussion of output in Chapter 5, I will use two types of input to illustrate the process of designing projects to improve input. These are the *services* and *products* that a team receives from internal or external suppliers. General examples of services are technical advice, delivery of goods, repair of equipment, and training programs. General examples of products are reports, budgets, and machined parts.

A training department in an organization receives inputs of data from various groups about training needs; it receives the names and files of job applicants from personnel; it receives advice about its budget from the comptroller; and it uses a variety of expendable materials obtained from supply. All these sources of input are *internal* suppliers.

At the same time, the training department might purchase a variety of instructional materials from various publishing houses, use the services of professional consultants, and contract for the use of special training or conference facilities. All these sources are *external* suppliers.

Internal and external suppliers differ along the same dimensions that distinguish internal customers from external ones: amount of power, type of power, and payoff. Teams typically will have more direct power over their external suppliers than they will over their internal ones. A training department, for example, may have the power to change its suppliers of instructional materials but probably will not have the power to change its source of personnel services. The payoffs for external suppliers are reputation, profit, and market share. The payoffs for internal suppliers are more diffused and subtle.

MAKING SUPPLIERS MEMBERS OF THE TEAM

It is obvious that, when a team is in the roles of processor and supplier, it will continually improve the satisfaction of its customers only if it takes the initiative to do so. When a team is in the role of customer, its own performance depends on its suppliers being motivated to improve the services and products that they deliver to the team. Put quite simply, teams that have undertaken to improve their own customers' satisfaction will want their suppliers to respond to them in the same way. Teams must consider, therefore, how to encourage their suppliers to become serious about satisfying their customers—the teams.

If customers have enough leverage, they simply can require that their suppliers demonstrate that they are committed to total quality and continuous improvement. Motorola, for example, now requires that its suppliers compete for the Malcolm Baldrige Award

(*Techknowledge,* 1989). The Department of Defense and the National Aeronautics and Space Administration are beginning to include total quality management as a criterion to qualify contractors and to evaluate them. Cadillac reversed its decline in market share and achieved the highest percentage of repeat buyers in the automobile industry largely through its implementation of simultaneous engineering (SE). A key to the success of SE was Cadillac's requirement that its external suppliers demonstrate continuous improvement in meeting targets for excellence in five areas: quality, cost, delivery, technology, and management. External suppliers obviously are under more pressure to be responsive to direction from their customers (especially major customers) than are internal suppliers. The rewards of profit, employment, and survival may depend on such responsiveness.

The rewards of profit, employment, and survival have less importance for internal suppliers than they do for external ones. Even these rewards have less day-to-day impact on the performance of external suppliers than do other factors.

One of the most significant strategies for influencing suppliers to improve their performance is for customers to include their suppliers on their teams. The conscious and deliberate practice of making suppliers a part of the team is an emerging practice in many organizations. This practice is most visible in relation to external suppliers.

When Brian Ehlers was developing the Apple Graphics Tablet, he recognized that he required the close support and help of his suppliers and included them on his design team. Summa Graphics, his major supplier, made over twenty-five prototypes before it created what Ehlers wanted. Summa Graphics was willing to do this because Ehlers made its people feel that they were part of the Apple team. The focus with Summa Graphics always was on solving problems and building a quality product, not on price. An indication of how much of a team Apple and Summa Graphics became is illustrated in the kind of help that Apple engineers gave to Summa Graphics. As a favor, Apple engineers redesigned one of the Summa

Graphics circuits, thereby improving the product that Summa Graphics sold to all its customers.

Another example is Hulki Aldikacti, Chief of Advanced Vehicle Design at Pontiac, who was responsible for designing and bringing to market Pontiac's Fiero. Aldikacti decided early in the project to make his suppliers part of his design and production team. His first step was to make the purchasing department part of his team. With that done, he was able to include key suppliers in the design process. One key role of the suppliers was to ensure that the design was compatible with available materials and manufacturing techniques.

By 1985, Cincinnati Milacron faced the fact that foreign suppliers had seized 50 percent of its market. The company formed a team with its suppliers to develop a new plastics-injection-molding machine. The goal was to build a machine that could produce a better quality product at greatly reduced costs. The team was a success, and Cincinnati Milacron has returned as a major player in its market. Although its suppliers knew the details of the new design, no information was ever leaked to Cincinnati Milacron's competitors during the entire design process (*Fortune*, 1990).

Over the past six years, I have been delivering a team-centered total quality management seminar for civil servants and contractors at NASA's Kennedy Space Center. The design of this seminar calls for members of the many different organizations to attend the seminar as teams. They may attend as management teams, intact work teams, project teams, or special teams. One practice that has developed over the years is for teams made up of suppliers and customers to attend. In some cases, NASA is present as the customer with one or more of its contractors (suppliers). In other cases, one contractor will be present as the customer with one or more of its subcontractors. Also present are teams made up of internal customers and suppliers. What has been demonstrated over and over again at the seminar (and in the follow-up studies we have made) is that:

1. Team development has a positive impact on performance and is the basis for continuous improvement regardless of the kind of group or team that is involved.

2. Certain characteristics of superior teams can be used as benchmarks and improvement targets regardless of the kind of team that uses them.

3. Team development is an appropriate strategy for improving the performance of suppliers.

The process of team development that we go through in the seminar permits several practical benefits to accrue to both the supplier and customer members of the team. Among such benefits are:

1. Customers begin to recognize just how important it is for them to help their suppliers to succeed. They also recognize that their suppliers want very much to succeed and to improve the satisfaction of their customers. Both supplier and customer perceive that they can succeed only as they succeed together and develop a win-win relationship.

2. Customers begin to realize the kinds of problems that they create for their suppliers that impede their performance. Such problems include poor direction, lack of timely feedback, very little positive feedback, and lack of objective criteria of performance evaluation.

3. Suppliers develop a commitment to their customers' success by understanding what these customers must do, in turn, to satisfy their own customers.

4. Both customers and suppliers develop a commitment to their joint development as a team.

5. Both customers and suppliers focus on solving problems rather than on ascribing blame. As they work as a team, they improve their skills in problem solving and in the use of a variety of rational problem-solving tools.

6. Finally, they discover that the roles of customer and supplier shift back and forth and that it helps performance to

understand and use this shift. For example, NASA is the customer with a large "C." But, at the working level, when a NASA team gives direction or technical advice to a contractor team, the contractor (at that moment) is a customer—albeit with a small "c." If the NASA team acts like a "supplier," it will do everything possible to help its "customer," and the prospect of improving the performance of the whole enterprise is greatly enhanced.

Team development can be undertaken by customer-supplier teams with the same model and tools that are described in Chapter 4: Improving and Measuring the Context of Team Development. The same sort of improvement projects that are described for work teams in Chapter 4 can be undertaken with customer-supplier teams.

The next section of this chapter will describe projects to improve input and customer performance. It will not specifically discuss team development projects for customer-supplier teams because sufficient information has been provided about such projects. *Team development, however, always should be considered the strategy of preference for continuous improvement within the work team, between the work team and its customers, and between the work team and its suppliers.*

PROJECTS TO IMPROVE INPUT AND SUPPLIER PERFORMANCE

In discussing projects to improve input and supplier performance, I will depart from the outline used in the previous three chapters, the six steps in the general design for improvement projects. By now the reader should be quite familiar with these six steps. Also, the reader should have an adequate knowledge of the TQM tools first introduced in Chapter 3.

It would be unnecessarily repetitious to describe the design of supplier-improvement projects with the same detail used for projects in the other three areas. Instead, this section will focus on the following:

- identifying suppliers,
- measuring the quality of suppliers' services and products, and
- keeping suppliers aware of the team's perceptions and expectations.

Designing projects to improve the performance of suppliers differs from other kinds of improvement projects in two significant ways. First, teams may find that they have a lot more freedom when designing projects to improve their own team development, their work processes, and the satisfaction of their customers than they do when they are designing projects to improve input and supplier performance. Second, a team may not be able to design with its suppliers a fully developed improvement project similar to the ones I have described. Suppliers may or may not choose to engage in a cooperative process of improvement with their customers. It is certainly to their advantage to do so, but (like anyone else) suppliers are not always capable of acting in their own best interests.

In short, suppliers can limit what customers can do. Customers, on occasion, may be able only to provide feedback to suppliers about the quality of their services and products. Customers may not always be able to help their suppliers to *improve* the quality of their services and products.

Identifying Suppliers

Before it can improve input and supplier performance, a team must know who its internal and external suppliers are. The next step is to determine whether there is any reason to set priorities for tracking or improving supplier performance, that is, are there current problems or opportunities for certain suppliers that should be addressed first? One of the TQM tools such as brainstorming or the nominal group technique might be used to identify the team's internal and external suppliers and those whose performance has the highest current priority.

There are two useful ways in which team members can categorize their suppliers to ensure that none are omitted. They might begin by developing two lists, one for internal suppliers and another for external suppliers. From these lists, they can identify the services and products that must be tracked. Or the team might list all the services and products that it uses and then attach the names of its suppliers to the various services and products. The following is a list of internal suppliers developed by a first-shift team in a metal shop. The team started by identifying inputs of services, information, and products that it used. Next, it prioritized the list and then it listed the internal suppliers associated with these inputs.

- The team in the shop that inputs partially machined parts;
- The third shift that turns over the process and work load to the first shift;
- The maintenance team that is responsible for the machines;
- The drafters and engineers who input the drawings and specifications;
- The human-resources pool that provides replacements when the team is short-handed;
- The training group that delivers skill training for new people and new machines;
- Shipping and Receiving, which delivers special tools and materials.

After a list of suppliers and their inputs has been identified (such as that of the metal shop), the next step is to determine how to measure these inputs so that they can be tracked and improved.

Measuring the Quality of Suppliers' Input (Services and Products) and Performance

From the customer's perspective, a supplier's performance is, first of all, a function of the *measured* quality of the service and product that it delivers. Customers will, however, determine quality not only by measuring an *objective* attribute such as thickness or whether a machine actually worked, they also will measure the quality of input with *subjective* criteria based on their perceptions and expectations. The process of improving supplier performance requires that teams help their suppliers to understand and respond to customers' perceptions and expectations.

Measuring Supplier Input

Teams must take four steps toward understanding the measured quality of the input they receive from suppliers:

- identify the input,
- establish the relative importance of all inputs,
- develop measures for tracking the quality of the input, and
- use the measures to track and improve the quality of the input.

The "Structured Process To Develop Measured Quality of Output," described in Chapter 5, can be adapted to identifying and measuring the quality of input.

The measures of quality that teams will need to establish for their inputs are *attribute* and *cost*. Attribute measures answer questions such as, "What is the ratio of errors to product or service unit?" and "What is the relation of failures to time of operation?" Cost measures answer questions such as, "How much was the purchase cost?" "How much did it cost (in training, installation, modification, unplanned delay) to make the product or service fit to use?" "How much did it cost to maintain and repair?" and "What was the actual cost compared to the promised cost?"

Examples of Measures of Cost

The method for developing measures of output described in Chapter 5 can be applied to developing measures of input related to cost. The basic model for this kind of measure is:

$$\frac{\text{Service or product unit}}{\text{Sources of cost}}$$

Here are a few ratios that a team might develop with its suppliers to measure costs of services and products:

$$\frac{\text{Unassembled equipment}}{\text{Hours to assemble}}$$

$$\frac{\text{Product}}{\text{Costs caused by delay in delivery}}$$

$$\frac{\text{Product unit}}{\text{Initial cost on delivery}}$$

$$\frac{\text{Machine units}}{\text{Annual maintenance cost}}$$

$$\frac{\text{\# of material units in inventory required for smooth production}}{\text{Cost to store}}$$

Examples of Measures of Attributes

The basic model for this measure is:

$$\frac{\text{Indicators of error, loss, or failure}}{\text{Service or product unit measured}}$$

A measure of attribute compares an output with data concerning error, loss, or failure. Here are a few ratios that a team might develop with its suppliers to measure attributes of services and products:

$$\frac{\text{Number of missing parts}}{\text{Units of unassembled equipment}}$$

$$\frac{\text{Errors in repair requests}}{\text{Number of requests}}$$

$$\frac{\text{Deliveries late}}{\text{Deliveries scheduled}}$$

$$\frac{\text{Number not qualified}}{\text{Number of applicants listed as qualified}}$$

$$\frac{\text{Number of units out of specification}}{\text{Batch}}$$

Ensuring that Suppliers Know Team's Perceptions and Expectations

Supplier performance is not just objective measures with ratios of costs and attributes. These ratios are useful in assessing supplier performance, but suppliers also must be informed regularly of the customer's perceptions and expectations. Perceptions and expectations in this context are similar to their role in helping the team as supplier to improve its customers' satisfaction. When the team is in the role of customer, it must take the initiative, as necessary, to ensure that its suppliers have regular and useable feedback about the team's perceptions and expectations. Feedback can be both formal and informal. Informal feedback is a function of contact and availability. Formal feedback will be in the shape of written assessments and evaluations.

Teams can initiate a variety of informal contacts with their suppliers. One electronics group that was responsible for supervising a contract for computer services set up a weekly meeting with an open agenda. Anyone who had a question or concern about present or future problems was invited to attend. The purpose was to clarify mutual expectations and provide mutual assistance. The results of each meeting were distributed to members of both the electronics and computer-services organizations.

I know of more than one team that has regular, morning telephone conferences with its principal suppliers to review problems and clarify priorities and expectations. Other teams organize exchange visits with their suppliers.

There is no substitute for frequent, direct, personal contact with suppliers. The fact is, however, that even within organizations, many customers have never visited the offices or shops of their internal suppliers.

A few months ago, a team of mechanics that attended a seminar of mine admitted that less than half of them had ever seen the shops that produced the products they designed. The team now requires that all its new engineers and drafters spend a week in each of the shops that they use during the first three months on the job. The team also requires that each engineer and drafter visit all the shops that they use at least once every week. The last time I talked to the supervisor of the engineering group, she reported that the results of these simple initiatives to stay in touch with suppliers "had been remarkable."

> We have a great deal less rework on our projects. We have found that the engineers and drafters now use the shops as resources, and it is quite usual now for an engineer to involve shop people early in the process of making a new design. We now have one team instead of the two or three competitive groups that we used to have who were always complaining about one another.

Supplier-Performance Index

There are all kinds of formal ways to assess suppliers and give them feedback on their performance (Fitzgibbons & Juran, 1974; Siegel, 1966). The simple process described in Chapter 5 under the title Customer-Satisfier Matrix can be applied by teams to give suppliers feedback about the team's perceptions of and expectations regarding supplier performance.

Figure 7-1 is an example of a supplier-performance matrix that a metal shop developed for one of its internal suppliers, the shipping and receiving department.

An examination of the Supplier-Performance Matrix in Figure 7-1 indicates that the metal shop gave shipping and receiving an overall rating of 36.50 out of a possible rating of 50.00. In other words, shipping and receiving was rated at 73 percent (36.50/50.00 x 100).

SATISFIERS	WEIGHT	RATING	WT. X RATING	WEIGHTED RATING
1. Deliveries complete	3	3.0	3 x 3.0	9.00
2. No damage	2	4.5	2 x 4.5	9.00
3. Deliveries on time	2	3.5	2 x 3.5	7.00
4. Promises kept	2	4.0	2 x 4.0	8.00
5. Cooperation	1	3.5	1 x 3.5	3.50
			SUMMARY RATING	36.50

**Figure 7-1. Supplier-Performance Matrix
for Shipping and Receiving**

The metal shop discussed the results of its matrix with shipping and receiving. The metal shop was most concerned with the "deliveries complete" category. It kept a record of the number of times that deliveries were incomplete and the loss of time that incomplete deliveries caused, i.e., setting up to start a job and then not being able to because the materials were not included in a scheduled delivery (although available in shipping and receiving) or being forced to stop a job because materials were not included in a delivery. The metal shop concluded that it had an average of thirty-two nonproductive hours per week because of incomplete deliveries. The metal shop also measured the percentage of deliveries that were incomplete. The shop's records indicated that 4.5 percent of its deliveries had been incomplete over the past thirty days.

Based on a mutual analysis of the metal shop's data (along with verifying data from shipping and receiving), shipping and receiving agreed to make the reduction of incomplete deliveries a specific improvement target. The metal shop proposed that a team consisting of members of both departments be established to resolve the problem. It further proposed that they set a target of reducing incomplete deliveries to 2 percent by the end of the next thirty-day period. This is a good example of a team taking the initiative to include a supplier in order to improve the supplier's performance.

SUMMARY

In this chapter, I have focused on the fourth area in which teams have opportunities for continuous improvement: input and supplier performance. I have addressed the following topics:

- The relationship of the other improvement areas to supplier performance;
- Differences between external and internal suppliers;
- Identifying suppliers;
- Making suppliers members of the team;
- Measuring the quality of suppliers' services and products; and
- Keeping suppliers aware of the team's perceptions and expectations.

The major point of this chapter is that supplier improvement, like all other significant improvement, is a result of team development and teamwork. The general strategy for improving supplier performance is for the customer to take the initiative to create the customer-supplier team.

Chapter  8

Getting Started: Strengthening the Capacity To Improve

The first seven chapters of this book describe how teams can conceptualize the process of continuous improvement and then set about the task of designing specific improvement projects. A rational model for undertaking continuous improvement has been presented. However, one of the realities in teams and organizations is that continuous improvement often is not very rational. Although teams may have no difficulty in using the model and tools described in this book, they often have difficulty in getting started. In this chapter, therefore, I address some of the issues that teams may face in getting started.

Continuous improvement is far from easy. One of the most difficult tasks that teams face is getting their members to *commit* to the task of continuous improvement. Teams also often find that (even though they may want to improve) they lack a basic prerequisite for improvement. They lack the *capacity to inquire.*

INQUIRY AND IMPROVEMENT

The most fundamental problem that organizations often must face in initiating TQM and continuous improvement is that they may have insufficient capacity to recognize and initiate opportunities to improve. Work teams that have been thoroughly socialized into organizations that do not stimulate and reinforce continuous improvement in every aspect of their structure will, to a greater or lesser degree, share this incapacity. I have concluded that this problem stems from an organizational learning disorder: *the inability to inquire.*

Inquiry is not the same as learning or problem solving, although it certainly is a component of these larger processes. In the most general sense, inquiry is the process of asking "why?," "how?," "what?," or "when?" For the purposes of this book, I have given it an even more limited meaning. I use the term to define that first step that we must take to identify the multitude of opportunities that exist in teams and organizations for improving quality. Inquiry (as it is related to continuous improvement) begins with the acknowledgement that all actions, processes, products, and services are continually aging and decaying. Understood this way, inquiry will exist in organizations to the degree that every question about actions, processes, products, and services is accepted as potentially useful.

Continuous improvement is, first of all, a function of inquiry. Inquiry is its precondition. *Continuous improvement will not take hold and survive in work teams or organizations until they are populated by people who are free to ask any question and make any suggestion about any aspect of their work.*

Of course, individual personality traits and internal mental blocks affect each person's degree of openness and ability to inquire. Argyris (1988) and Senge (1990) have suggested that our capacity to inquire and learn is limited because we have inadequate mental models. Some thirty years ago, Rokeach (1960) proposed that the lack of openness (as the inability to entertain alternatives) was a correlate of personality traits such as authoritarianism and dogmatism.

I do not discount the effect that personality traits may have on inquiry. There obviously is considerable interaction between the personal capacity of an individual for inquiry and the willingness to use that capacity in a specific work environment. But, apart from our individual characteristics and idiosyncracies, the impediments to inquiry that exist *in our teams and organizations* have a profound impact on how free we are to inquire.

There are considerable data to support the assertion that people in work teams and organizations often do not feel free to inquire (Argyris, 1988, 1990; Argyris & Schon, 1978; Lindblom, 1990). If inquiry is considered to be a component of creativity, then studies on creativity provide additional support for the assertion (Twiss, 1986).

We probably do not need to look beyond our own experience for sufficient corroboration of the assertion that people in organizations often do not feel free to inquire. If we are to foster continuous improvement, we must nurture inquiry and make it as easy as possible for people to question everything that they do and see.

At least two kinds of impediments to inquiry are present in most organizations and work teams. The first is a set of organizational *conditions* that often are unexamined and whose influence, therefore, is unacknowledged. The second kind of impediment is a set of *communication* habits that organizations have accepted and reinforced for so long that they have become the norm.

CONDITIONS IN ORGANIZATIONS AND TEAMS THAT BLOCK INQUIRY

Organizations create their own cultures of values, beliefs, norms, and practices. Like all other social institutions, organizations tend to create convergent thinking and to limit inquiry (Harvey, 1988; Jewell & Airey, 1984; Lindblom, 1990; Spence, 1978).

The degree to which the cultures of organizations affect the values and thinking processes of their members has been communicated repeatedly to me during one of my long-term consulting relationships. Over the past fifteen years, while working in an environment composed of a government agency and its contractors, I have been able to observe the power of organizational culture. I have seen people move from the government agency to take employment with one of its contractors or move from one contractor to another. I am always surprised at just how quickly these people change their beliefs and practices. When they are with the government agency, the contractors are the enemies. When they are employed by a contractor, the government is the enemy. When they move from contractor A to contractor B, contractor A becomes an enemy. Not only do these people change their values and attitudes, but they remain largely unaware that they have changed them.

Socialization is the process by which organizations ensure that their employees "fit." This process is accomplished by means of all sorts of formal and informal, explicit and implicit actions (Ritti & Funkhouser, 1982). The positive side of the socialization process in organizations is that it contributes a degree of order and stability to people's lives and to the total organization. People learn what to expect, and the result is continuity and reliability. When people are not successfully socialized into the central values, norms, and behaviors of an organization, they feel alienated and can become unproductive.

The negative side of socialization is that it can block inquiry and threaten the organization's ability to learn and survive. An organization's process of socialization can lead to abject subservience and conformity in its members and work teams to norms and values that ultimately may be counter to the organization's best interests or even its survival.

If teams are to undertake continuous improvement, they must create the possibility for improvement first by understanding the conditions that tend to block inquiry and then by turning these blocks into improvement opportunities. The conditions that I have observed to be the most pervasive and serious blocks to inquiry are:

- values,

- rules,

- roles,

- membership, and

- elitism.

There is, no doubt, some degree of overlap among these five categories, and there are probably additional categories that will occur to the reader. Nevertheless, I have found that these categories seem to be true for most members of the teams and organizations with which I work. Moreover, these categories help teams and organizations to identify and overcome their blocks to inquiry and continuous improvement.

Values

The most general problem that we face in undertaking improvement is that we fail to recognize or initiate opportunities to improve. The executives, managers, and employees that I work with usually are willing to respond to problems that represent a deficit (e.g., deviations such as delays in processing time, machinery breakdowns, increased costs, loss of market share, and increase in personnel turnover). They expend great energy in solving problems *after* they occur. Their value to their organizations largely is determined by their reputation for being people who can solve such problems.

However, what these executives, managers, and employees do *not* do very well is spend time anticipating and solving problems in performance or production *before* they occur. They do not accept the challenge to improve what already works. Of course, their organizations do not reward them for solving these kinds of problems.

In some organizations, even the term "improvement" is not fully acceptable. Some years ago, I was asked to design a "Productivity-Improvement" seminar for the E Organization. The first obstacle that I faced was that everyone—from the chief executive officer to the members of the training staff—wanted me to find a title for the seminar that did not include the words "productivity" and "improvement!"

Continuous improvement is not an expectation that is built into the underlying value system of most organizations (Kinlaw,

1991). The explicit message that is communicated daily to most people is that they should do their jobs. This message is reinforced in many formal and informal ways.

- People are rewarded most for simply doing their jobs, not for improving how their jobs are done.
- Continuous improvement is not mentioned in job descriptions.
- Continuous improvement is not included as an evaluation point in the performance plans of managers and other employees.
- When people are hired into new jobs, it rarely is emphasized that they are expected to add value to every aspect of their jobs and to improve every system and operation.
- The training budgets of organizations rarely emphasize continuous improvement, and people rarely are provided with sufficient team development, analytical, or statistical skills to undertake continuous improvement.
- Organizations rarely require work groups to devote time to improvement, and in many cases employees find strong resistance when their teams meet to work on improvement opportunities.

The advent of TQM has generated new interest in strategies for increasing employee influence, such as employee-suggestion systems, but the focus of most suggestion systems reveals just how strong traditional values are and how inadequate our understanding of continuous improvement is. Employee-suggestion programs usually operate within hierarchical systems of control that:

- Include many administrative and approval steps that cause lengthy delays between the time an employee makes a suggestion and the time he or she receives a response;

- Use acceptance criteria that restrict suggestions to what are considered part of the employee's normal job responsibilities; and

- Require involved evaluation to determine the dollar value to the company.

The result of these controls is that suggestion systems generate a limited number of ideas rather than the greatest possible number of improvement ideas.

Another illustration of how organizational values inhibit inquiry is that they do little to cultivate "playfulness." They do not encourage people to try "what if?" or "let's pretend." The orientation of organizations toward short-term results, the rigid control of job behaviors, and the practical bias toward getting the job done all breed serious-mindedness. Playful exploration has been identified by a number of authors as an ingredient of innovation, improvement, problem solving, and creativity (Campbell, 1985; Taylor, 1964). We can expect that organizations that do not value improvement will not value inquiry, and they certainly will not value play.

One condition that team members must address as they take up the challenge of continuous improvement is the effect that its operating values may have on the team's ability and willingness to inquire. We cannot reasonably expect ourselves and others to develop the habit of continuous improvement if we do not identify the values that inhibit inquiry and take action to limit their influence.

Modifying the values that operate in our teams, as well as the other conditions and behaviors that limit inquiry, can be accomplished best through team action. At the end of this section are several team strategies for changing these blocks into improvement opportunities.

Rules

A second condition that blocks inquiry is the existence of rules (often unarticulated and unwritten) that keep many potentially useful questions from being asked.

"Centralization is necessary for economies of scale." "Pay when the invoice is received." "Large-batch processing is the most efficient." "Only engineers are qualified to make designs." "Customers should not repair their own machines." "Inventory is necessary to ensure stable production processes." All these rules have developed from earlier periods of time in which very different business and manufacturing conditions prevailed. All these rules evolved before the advent of instant information, relational data bases, and computer networking. A variety of companies have shown that these rules can be challenged successfully and have replaced them with new rules—ones that properly reflect current business and technological conditions.

Take, for example, the rules "Inventory is necessary to ensure stable production processes" and "Large-batch processing is the most efficient." Taiichi Ono questioned the need for inventory and large-batch processing when he observed how American supermarkets function. He observed that the American customer "pulled" the groceries through the system. Stores were resupplied daily and did not maintain large supplies of inventory (*Fortune*, 1990). By questioning the requirement for inventory, Ono and Toyota created just-in-time inventory (JIT). JIT is customer driven, it permits the profitable manufacture of small batches of products, and it reduces the costs that are generated when any item in a process must be delayed by storage, i.e., placed in inventory.

Or take the rule, "Pay when the invoice is received." This one rule leads companies to employ large numbers of people in their accounts payable departments. The rule drives a process that has at least the following steps: purchasing writes an order, and a copy is sent to accounts payable; when receiving has the ordered item on the dock, it sends a receiving document to accounts payable; accounts payable matches the purchase order with the receiving document; when accounts payable receives an invoice from the supplier, it pays the bill.

The Ford Motor Company questioned the rule and instituted invoiceless processing. In the new process, purchasing places an order and enters the information in an on-line database. When receiving has the shipment, it checks the database, verifies the order, and enters its acceptance into the database. A check is issued automatically (Hammer, 1990).

Rules, like values, can hinder inquiry. So can roles.

Roles

A third condition that often limits inquiry in organizations and teams comprises the roles that members occupy. When a person takes a job, he or she begins to take on a role. The person takes on defined responsibilities and expected behaviors and develops a sense of personal identity with the job. We "become" secretaries, managers, technicians, consultants, purchasing agents, pipe fitters, and press operators. We also develop a strong sense of what people in our jobs do and do not do. We accept finite areas of responsibility and the boundaries to action that accompany our roles.

Roles have fences. When strong role identities develop, people learn to stay within their fences and they learn to expect others to stay within their fences.

Role identification fragments vision and curiosity. It has a negative impact on inquiry. Role identification encourages us to be concerned only with our own jobs; we often do not understand how our jobs interact with others. Role identification makes it a virtue to "mind one's own business." The negative impact of role identification can be heard in exchanges such as the following:

1. *Supervisor:* "Why didn't you stop and think before you sent out that form letter?"
   Clerk: "That's not my job. You're paid to think; I'm paid to follow the procedure."

2. *First Worker:* "Didn't you see that I was using an uncalibrated tool? Why didn't you stop me?"
   Second Worker: "It's not my job to stop anyone. You're supposed to do your job, and I'm supposed to do mine."

3. *Staff Member:* "I thought we were all here to figure this out together and decide what is best."

Manager: "I'm getting paid to make the decisions. I know that the rest of you think you know better. My job is to make the decisions, and your job is to carry them out."

To improve the quality of performance, we must be able to stimulate and recognize opportunities for improvement. A first step is to identify the conditions that may have subtle and unrecognized influences on us and which limit our capacity to inquire. Two such blocks stem from the values and rules that exist in our organizations and teams. Another block comes from the roles that we have taken on with our jobs. A fourth block is one of the effects of membership.

Membership

Membership in groups often is paid for by the high price of thinking what the group thinks and conforming to how other members behave. We all are familiar with stories about peer pressure and the danger of being "rate busters." But we may not be aware that the power of membership can keep us from asking questions and looking for new improvement opportunities.

Organization F knows that you cannot get good information from surveys. Surveys give employees an opportunity to gripe. No self-respecting member of Organization F would ever suggest that a survey could be used to diagnose the organization's health.

An organization that requires its members to believe that "if it wasn't invented here, it doesn't work" prevents them from inquiring about the relative merits of other approaches, processes, techniques, and products; it demands that they persist in the wasteful and tedious process of reinventing almost everything.

In some organizations, the price of membership on the management team is complete agreement (or lack of visible disagreement) with the CEO. Because membership on the management team represents one's continued employment, very few managers press the issue.

In other organizations, the requirements for membership in a department or team are unique to that part of the organization and may not be known to the organization. These can be among the most insidious requirements of membership. They may represent the preferences of a manager or the "old-timers" on the team, or they may have grown out of the personalities of the original team members.

Inquiry is the foundation for learning, and it is only a learning organization that can expect to survive in a period of global competition, market instability, and accelerated information exchange (Argyris & Schon, 1978; de Geus, 1988; Stata, 1989). *One goal that every team and every organization should have, therefore, is that the freedom to inquire and the willingness to learn (above all else) become the primary norms for membership.*

Elitism

A fifth condition that blocks inquiry is the belief that the elite know best. The elite in organizations belong to a variety of subgroups. They may be the executives and managers or the people who have been around the longest. They may be the people with the most advanced degrees or the corporate staff people who have the ear of the chief executive. The elite are the people who make decisions and shape opinion. They also may shape conformity and limit inquiry.

It is easy to identify the elite. Every time a new idea is introduced or an improvement is proposed, the opinions and decisions of the elite hold sway. They rarely are challenged.

The general supervisor of a group of boiler makers and pipe fitters is convinced that his people should receive training in human relations so that they will treat one another with consideration and respect. At the beginning, a few foremen indicate that the problem is that no one is rewarded for being nice. They point out that people are not rewarded much at all. They are, however, punished if jobs are not finished on time, and the general supervisor carries the biggest stick and uses it freely. Over time, the disbelieving foremen are weeded out. The general supervisor and the foremen soon speak with one voice. The opinion of the elite is that people need human relations training. The training persists over several years. Nothing is improved, but the opinion of the elite persists. Eventually the organization becomes known as one that "believes" in human relations training.

In Organization N, the chief executive and his staff are presented the results of an organizational survey. One key finding is that there is poor upward and downward communication. The chief pronounces that "communication is always a problem in all organizations." From then on, it is known that communication always will be a problem that cannot be fixed and can, therefore, be ignored.

In hospitals, the doctors are the elite; they are permitted to pronounce on any issue—whether it has to do with medicine or not. In some organizations, the elite are the people with advanced degrees (whose knowledge may be very specialized); in others, they are the people at corporate headquarters.

It is the task of any elite to protect its privileged position. It is hardly surprising to find that the executive and managerial elite of most organizations unequivocally affirm that hierarchical structures and differences in rank, status, and prestige are necessary (Verba & Orren, 1985). Research has, however, made it very clear that the traditional hierarchy is not the best way to foster open communication, team development, creativity, and continuous improvement (Argyris, 1990).

It also is clear that the self-serving needs of any elite can inhibit inquiry. It often is a punishing experience to question the wisdom of the elite. The elite can turn the act of asking questions into one of disloyalty and subversion.

One executive whom I have observed for a long time talks a lot about teamwork and being a team player. What he really means is that he is the owner, coach, and quarterback, and that to be a team player means to do as he says. Time and time again, I have seen people on his staff adopt the survival strategy of waiting for this executive to pronounce on any topic before they speak. At the same time, in private, this executive often has complained to me that his subordinates do not seem to have many new ideas!

The people in organizations who have the best ideas about how to improve a process or operation may not be the most forceful. The more defined and vocal the elite groups are, the more push is required from people who are not members of the elite if they are to get a fair hearing for their ideas.

The first block to inquiry consists of conditions that operate in organizations and teams: values, rules, roles, membership, and elitism. The second is communication habits.

COMMUNICATION HABITS THAT BLOCK INQUIRY

Inquiry in organizations and teams is inhibited by *communication habits* that readily can be observed during conversations and team meetings. These habits often have become so accepted that they are modeled by the organization's most successful people. The habits are the reactions that one person exhibits to an idea, opinion, or suggested improvement offered by another person. These responses tend to transform an interaction from an investigative dialogue or discussion into an argument—or they simply shut down any attempt to exchange information from which new insight might evolve.

The following catalog of communication habits that block inquiry certainly is not complete; nevertheless, it does identify some of the behaviors that are the most common and destructive. These communication habits are categorized as follows:

- focusing on exceptions or faults,
- responding with irrelevancies,
- data-free thinking, and
- jumping to solutions.

Focusing on Exceptions or Faults

Pointing out exceptions and finding faults (e.g., identifying potential problems or undesirable results) are ways to deflect suggestions for change or improvement. This type of response blocks inquiry and does not encourage further exploration. It shifts the focus away from the purpose of the suggested improvement or its positive aspects.

For example, an employee suggests that a training program be established for people who might want to be supervisors and who would like to find out what the job is all about. The personnel manager objects with the exception, "But then some people will think that they are being groomed to be supervisors." In another example, a consultant proposes that a survey be made to determine the degree to which managers and supervisors understand their roles and responsibilities in the company's TQM initiative. One manager objects that the survey "might embarrass some managers because it will point out so much that they are not doing." Obviously, the managers in these examples have created blocks to the thoughtful and careful *consideration* of the merits of the proposed improvements.

Here is another example. A proposal is made to introduce a team-focused rewards system to encourage the development of teams and to reinforce the concept that teamwork is the key to superior performance. The response is a litany of objections.

- "Individuals will feel slighted."
- "We will discourage individual achievement and hard work."
- "The unions will never accept it."
- "You will never convince our supervisors that it will work."
- "It will make it too easy for nonperformers to get lost in the team."
- "We will end up rewarding the high and low performers the same way."

All these objections may be true or may make sense, but they still do not address the need for team-focused rewards. They are premature objections that make it almost impossible to explore whatever positive attributes might be associated with a team-based reward system.

One discipline that must be learned by anyone who is serious about improvement is to *concentrate first on the potential usefulness of an idea rather than on its possible limitations.*

Responding with Irrelevancies

A second common and observable behavior that blocks inquiry is responding with irrelevancies. This is the process of objecting to an idea, proposal, or improvement by introducing material that is beside the point or inconsequential.

I once made a presentation to a group of managers about the process for developing superior teams. My assumption was that the topic was timely and that the participants would have a lively interest in it. At the first coffee break, I was completely taken aback when one participant asked, "Did you know that you used the word 'ain't' four times this morning?" I thought that we were in the midst of discussing the fundamental strategy to regain our competitive edge, and one manager was keeping track of how many times I used "ain't!" (I had used the word in the context of relating verbatim several stories about superior teams.)

I have observed senior managers listen to a presentation on a key issue and then take issue with the presenters because the view graphs were "too attractive," or "not attractive enough."

For twelve years, I have given a workshop on interpersonal communication for managers in a particular organization. During the workshop, the managers participate in a video-interactive exercise in which they practice the process and skills that they are learning. They are then asked to identify their key learnings from the exercise. Without exception, one or more of these participants will not describe what he or she has learned but will describe how the design of the exercise should be changed. Over the years, I have redesigned the exercise to try to take into consideration each of the comments that I have received. But no matter how much or how often the exercise has been redesigned, still (after twelve years) I see comments on how to redesign the exercise rather than the requested statement about learnings. I have concluded that responding with irrelevancies is a technique of many people in this organization; some of them always will focus not on what is central and important but on what is tangential or peripheral. Perhaps it is a way of avoiding the need to speak knowledgeably about the central issue. Whatever the reason for this habit, if it is unchallenged, it will continue to block inquiry and prevent the team or organization from exploring new and potentially better ways of doing things.

Data-Free Thinking

There are a number of synonyms for data-free thinking: making unfounded assumptions, generalizing, labeling, and leaping to abstractions. The effect of these behaviors is to divert people from the difficult task of thinking concretely. An even more destructive result is that data-free thinking encourages people to imagine that they know something when they really do not.

Most of the performance-appraisal systems that I have examined over the years illustrate the danger of generalizations and abstractions. I have seen evaluation categories such as "responsiveness," "cooperativeness," "independence," "sensitivity to others," and "professionalism" included in a variety of appraisal forms. The danger of such indefinite descriptors is twofold: (a) they do not contain real information for people to use, but (b) they encourage people to think and act as though they did have real information. Once I decide that a person is not "responsive," or "cooperative," or "professional," that decision will influence all kinds of other decisions on my part.

When our opinions and decisions are data-free, they are impossible to debate, and they certainly inhibit serious inquiry. The automobile industry in this country provides an example of data-free thinking carried out on a grand scale. The Detroit automobile manufacturers operated for years on data-free opinions—long after these opinions clearly were leading them into serious difficulty. As late as the mid-seventies, these companies still operated on the assumption that foreign manufacturers never would be a real threat because Americans preferred big cars; big cars meant big profits; and only Detroit made big cars (Halberstam, 1986). These companies persisted with other data-free opinions (until they were on the brink of disaster), such as: don't do it first, let the other fellow make the expensive mistake; people want to change their cars every two or three years, so obsolescence is good; price is more important than quality; and management knows best.

Recently I was asked to work with a small company that was providing a variety of contract-personnel services to other companies in its area. During my second week with this company, it lost a bid to renew one of its largest existing contracts. In my first meeting with the principals of the company (after it had received the news about losing the contract), there took place a lengthy discussion about why the company had lost the contract. After a fairly wild period in which people suggested that the cause was political, or that there were just too many competitors, or that the other company just wanted to make a change, the group agreed that the reason was cost. The principals were convinced that they had been underbid and that cost (not quality) was paramount in the client company's decision.

At this point, there was not one shred of concrete information to suggest that the company had lost the bid because of cost. The group had no information on which to base *any* opinion. The people at the meeting seemed to be operating on the assumption that "We provide the best quality service in the area, therefore the only reason that we could have lost the contract is cost."

The danger to this group and the company was that its data-free opinion could have sidetracked it away from the real problem, that of a lost client. Left to itself, this company would not have looked at its own performance and targeted real opportunities to improve. As is true of most organizations, once this company began to analyze its own performance, it began to uncover one opportunity for improvement after another. It even found out that it had not fulfilled several provisions of the contract it had lost.

The suggestion that managers and supervisors should practice more participative management has been around for a long time. This idea has undergone something of a rebirth as TQM has begun to catch on. One simple way to understand participative management and translate it into action is to get managers and supervisors to extend more influence to their employees, e.g., to give them the chance to offer new ideas, to solve problems, and to become involved in a variety of decision-making opportunities.

One of the recurring data-free opinions that I encounter in each of the seminars that I teach on participative management is that "people do not want to be involved." The predominant amount of research information actually indicates that people *do* want to be involved. But, so long as these managers and supervisors persist in their data-free opinion, they will make many errors that will inhibit improvement in the performance of their work teams and organizations. The biggest inhibitor is that they will not figure out how to use to the fullest advantage the mental resources that their people represent.

Jumping to Solutions

Recently, I was asked to assist a mental-health-care unit to identify opportunities for improvement. I introduced the group to the Model for Continuous Improvement and Measurement (Figure 2-1) and then led it through a structured process for identifying opportunities for improvement. We had data on some of the systems that the group used to manage appointments and client followup, so I suggested that we start with one of these systems. The group, however, had a very difficult time focusing on its opportunities for improvement. One reason was that each time a problem was introduced, someone immediately would offer a solution. What began to happen, of course, was that when one person offered a solution, others reacted to the solution rather than trying to understand the opportunity for improvement. Here is an example of a typical interchange in the group.

Member A: "It looks like we could decrease the number of people who don't show up for their scheduled appointments."

Member B: "Why don't we contact each person the day before the appointment and double check."

Member C: "It would probably help to have the intake clerk complete a preliminary description of the client's problem while the client is on the phone. That would make the client take the appointment more seriously."

Member D: "I think that we might run into some liability or legal problems if we used intake clerks to take information about some personal problem or symptoms."

Member C: "We could check that out with legal. But I don't think that would work anyhow. It would just be another time-consuming operation."

And so the discussion rambled on. A variety of solutions were discussed without the problem ever being fully understood. The result was quite predictable. No strategies were developed, and the subject was tabled.

I believe wholeheartedly in the need for training in organizations, but training is not the answer to everything. One of the frequent examples of jumping to solutions is the ease and promptness with which people in organizations conclude that their problem (whatever it is) can be solved by training. The unstated bias, of course, is that most problems are people problems. The litany of these people problems and their "solutions" goes something like this:

- Our managers don't stay in touch with their people. They need to learn how to be friendly and talk to their people.

- Our supervisors don't show respect for their people. They need to learn how to be less caustic and critical.

- Our supervisors are not getting the performance appraisals of their people to personnel on time. They need to be taught how important the appraisal is and how it should be completed.

- Our people are leaving the tags off the valves and switches that flag the ones that cannot be opened without higher authority. We need to run them all through another indoctrination class on how to tag equipment.

I once made a study of improvement opportunities for the TQM council of a corporation. One desire that was expressed by the field offices was that corporate headquarters take the initiative to establish improvement teams at critical interfaces where the responsibilities for systems and processes were shared by two or more field offices. One member of the council indicated that there already was a system for reporting interface problems to corporate and that if people just used this system, these interface problems would be handled. Once this was said, the council pursued the issue no further. The solution proved to be no solution. The problem went unresolved because it never had been understood.

I now have identified two general categories of inhibitors that block inquiry and that can frustrate any attempt at continuous improvement.

The *organizational conditions* that inhibit inquiry are:

- values,
- rules,
- roles,
- membership, and
- elitism.

The *communication habits* that inhibit inquiry are:

- focusing on exceptions or faults,
- responding with irrelevancies,

- data-free thinking, and

- jumping to solutions.

At the end of this chapter, I will outline a few strategies for turning the blocks to inquiry into positive opportunities for improvement. Before that, I will enter one caution about the way we address improvement, in order to help the reader to avoid at least one major trap in the process of continuous improvement.

BLOCKS TO IMPROVEMENT ARE NOT RESISTANCES TO CHANGE

It has been fashionable for some years to consider change and the resistance to change as major organizational problems. It is tempting, therefore, just to consider continuous improvement as one more example of change for which there are a variety of resistances in the organization that must be overcome. I do not think, however, that resistance to change has proven to be a very useful concept in helping teams to plan and initiate continuous improvement. I have chosen, therefore, to discard it.

Although change and the resistance to change have been researched and written about extensively, it is questionable that much real progress has been made in solving the problems of change and resistance (Drucker, 1974). I have deliberately selected the term "blocks" rather than "resistances" to describe the conditions and communication habits that often exist in teams and organizations when they begin to plan and initiate continuous improvement.

I believe that the problems of change and resistance often are not solved because we are using concepts and categories that lead us to misunderstand the problem, or to misstate the problem, or to state the problem in such cosmological terms that it is unsolvable. There are at least two biases inherent in the traditional discussion of the resistance to change:

- Resistance is a function of individual feelings, fears, and biases.

- Resistance must be reduced before the desired change can take place.

The first effect of these two biases is that we can spend a lot of time and energy cataloging people's resistances to change (e.g., fear of losing security, money, job satisfaction, friends and associates, freedom, responsibility, authority, status, etc.). The second effect of these biases is that they encourage us to spend time developing data about the resistances we have cataloged (typically through an employee-attitude survey). Finally, these biases lead us to develop strategies to overcome the resistances rather than strategies for continuous improvement and measurement.

In addition to these biases and their effects, using resistances to change as a way of thinking about continuous improvement creates other negative results. The categories of resistance are as numerous as the people who have written about them (cf. Kirkpatrick, 1985; Lippitt, Langseth, & Mossop, 1985; Michael, 1981; Tichy, 1983). Also, more confusion has been created because:

- Lists of resistances to change derived from one point of view are generalized and applied in other points of view, e.g., categories of individual resistance are applied to groups and whole organizations, and categories of organizational resistance are applied to groups and individuals; and

- Strategies for managing resistances to change derived from one organizational level are applied inappropriately to other levels, e.g., strategies for the total organization are applied to smaller organizational units.

Having observed and monitored hundreds of groups as they have planned and successfully initiated continuous improvement, I have concluded that the correct way to define the problem of institutionalizing continuous improvement is to use concepts and categories that make the problem resolvable. *To do this means to always focus on how to make continuous improvement the norm rather than how to overcome resistances to continuous improvement.*

Here is one simple illustration of focusing on improvement rather than focusing on resistances to change. An activity that I have used for the past five years in one of my TQM seminars is to have teams identify blocks to their performance. When I first started using the activity, teams invariably would identify most of their blocks as problems or conditions caused by a person or group *outside* the team, such as managers, corporate headquarters, Japanese competitors, the union, and the government. It was only after I began to give the instruction that the teams were to "identify blocks that they caused or that they could remove" that the teams began to focus on what *they* could do to improve their performance.

I do not believe that the people in my seminars were resisting change. I also do not believe that diverting our interest to overcome these "resistances" would have accomplished anything. I believe that the people simply had a few dysfunctional thinking habits that were overcome by getting them to think about the problem of improvement in a different way.

Blocks to continuous improvement should not be viewed as resistances to change. Blocks are conditions and habits, both of which manifest themselves as behaviors. Our strategy should be to develop, practice, and reward the behaviors that we want and to make all other behaviors out of bounds.

A general strategy for turning blocks into opportunities is to:

1. Use them to assess a team's capacity for undertaking continuous improvement; and

2. Plan strategies for continuous improvement that take these blocks into account.

TEAM ACTION

Teams are the primary units of performance and production. The team, in all its variety, is the place where continuous improvement must take root and grow. The team is the place where the blocks to inquiry operate daily, and it is here that they can be examined most carefully.

There probably are an unlimited number of ways in which teams can turn the blocks to inquiry into improvement opportunities. The following are a few strategies that I have found particularly useful.

Strategy #1: Using the Set of Organizational Conditions

One useful strategy is to discuss the five conditions that limit inquiry and identify the degree to which these conditions exist in the team. Listed below are some questions that can be used to analyze each of the five conditions. After each condition has been examined, list: (a) the things that the team intends to *stop* doing that now reinforce the condition, and (b) the things that it intends to *start* doing to overcome the condition.

From the specific information developed in the discussion, the team can create norms that define what members expect of themselves and of one another.

Questions for Exploring the Impact of Values

Questions that can help a team to examine how team or organizational values block inquiry are:

1. How do we reward people for making improvements?
2. How much time do we set aside to work specifically on improving and measuring our performance?
3. What are some recent examples of our improving something "that wasn't broken?"
4. What are our specific improvement goals or objectives?

Questions for Exploring the Impact of Roles

Questions that can help a team to examine how the roles of members block inquiry are:

1. How do we ensure that we improve the way one job fits with another job?
2. What are examples of team members' failing to help or take action because "it wasn't my job?"
3. How do we ensure that we obtain new ideas from people in other disciplines, trades, and organizations?
4. How do we initiate joint problem solving between ourselves and people in other groups and jobs?
5. How do we test the ways in which we look at problems with the ways that other trades, groups, and disciplines look at their problems?
6. When have any of us backed off from trying to improve some aspect of our organization's performance or product because we didn't think it was part of our jobs?
7. When have we dismissed an idea because it came from a different shop, department, or work group?

Questions for Exploring the Impact of Membership

1. What do we think that we do better than any other work team or organization? How do we know? How have we tested ourselves?
2. How do we react when we are criticized by other people or teams? Do we respond defensively? Do we regard criticism as a possible opportunity for improvement?
3. Do we protect one another from the "truth?" To what degree are we honest with fellow team members when we believe that they are not doing quality work? How do we handle this?

Questions for Exploring the Impact of Elitism

1. What are some instances in which any of us deferred uncritically to people who were supposed to know more than we know?

2. Do we listen for the boss' opinion before we give our own?
3. How safe do we feel in disagreeing with our boss or with more senior people?
4. What opinions from "higher" or "more competent" authorities do we now accept uncritically?

Strategy #2: Using Team-Meeting Norms

Overcoming communication blocks to inquiry requires observation, feedback, and practice. Team meetings present an excellent opportunity to do this. Here are some recommended steps:

1. Discuss the behaviors that block inquiry and make the avoidance of these behaviors norms for team meetings. Examples of possible norms are:

   - Listen to and explore all ideas and understand them before we offer exceptions or identify possible faults;

   - Avoid responding to one another with irrelevancies;

   - Make no decisions that are not based on data; and

   - Make sure that everyone fully understands a problem before discussing solutions.

2. Decide how the norms will be enforced. When the team first uses norms, they should be enforced immediately (in real time) when the deviations occur and they should be assessed at the end of each meeting. As time goes on, it usually is sufficient to assess conformance to the team's norms at the end of meetings.

Strategy #3: Surveying the Team's Capacity for Inquiry

Teams often find it useful to conduct surveys in order to accumulate data to be discussed by the team members. The survey can give a team a "fix" on where it is and what it needs to do to foster inquiry and improvement. (An example of such a survey is included in the Appendix.) Teams may, of course, develop their own surveys.

Another option is not to actually administer a survey but to use survey questions in a team discussion. How each team will proceed will depend on the level of team development that already exists in the team.

CONCLUSION

Continuous improvement of quality no longer is a matter of choice for American business and industry. Continuous improvement has been mandated by global competition and the exponential expansion of information and technology. It is now a matter of survival.

There is now an enormous effort within most American organizations to improve quality. Much of it is well-founded, but much of it still amounts to a lot of posturing, window dressing, slogan-making, and banner-waving. The leaders of organizations persist in looking for some programmatic magic to save them.

Continuous improvement requires a lot of help in order to take hold and thrive in an organization. It requires strategic planning, management commitment, resources, and appropriate organizational structure. None of these factors, however, actually produces improvement. Nor do TQM "techniques" account for continuous improvement.

Continuous improvement becomes "real" as an ongoing, day-to-day process when it becomes a way of life for work teams. Continuous improvement is the direct result of teams (in all the different ways that they can exist) undertaking specific improvement projects.

The primary source of continuous improvement is teams. In this book, I have provided teams with a model and the tools for undertaking continuous improvement and measurement projects in four key areas: (a) team development; (b) output and customer satisfaction; (c) work processes; and (d) input and supplier performance. I challenge teams to use the freedom that they already possess, to act, and to measure their actions.

Appendix: TQM Tools and Examples

This Appendix contains four sections:

- Section 1: Models,
- Section 2: Rational/Structured Tools,
- Section 3: Numerical/Statistical Tools, and
- Section 4: Record-Keeping and Tracking Tools.

SECTION 1: MODELS

Models serve as tools for total quality management and continuous improvement in a number of ways.

1. They provide teams with a common conceptual basis for understanding improvement. For example, the Model for Continuous Improvement and Measurement (Figure 2-1) provides teams with a picture of the main areas of opportunity for improvement and the basis from which teams can build a common perception of improvement.

2. They can suggest to teams optional strategies for improvement. For example, the Model of Improvement Strategies (Figure 1-1) can be used by teams to ensure that they have a balanced set of improvement initiatives that are proactive as well as reactive.

This section includes one model in addition to those already mentioned in this book, the Model for Superior Team Development and Performance. A full description of this model is found in *Developing Superior Work Teams* (Kinlaw, 1991).

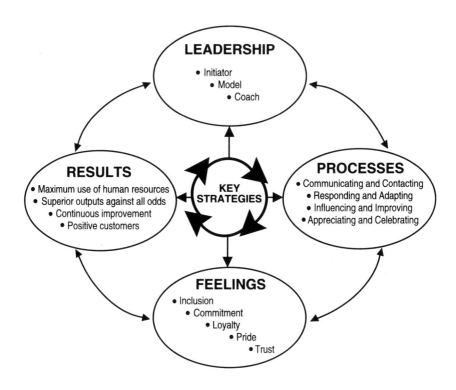

**Figure A-1. The Model For Superior Team
Development and Performance**

Reprinted with the permission of Lexington Books, an imprint of Macmillan,
Inc., from SUPERIOR WORK TEAMS: BUILDING QUALITY AND THE
COMPETITIVE EDGE, by Dennis C. Kinlaw. Copyright © 1991 by
Lexington Books.

The four primary elements in the model are:

1. **Achieving Superior Team Results.** These are the *final* outcomes: making maximum use of the team's human resources; delivering outputs of superior services and products (even against all odds); showing continuous improvement; and creating enthusiastically positive customers.

2. **Helping Team Processes To Emerge.** These processes are the *day-to-day*, informal processes of communicating and contacting, responding and adapting, influencing and improving, and appreciating and celebrating.

3. **Nurturing Positive Team Feelings.** Among the most important feelings are those of inclusion, commitment, loyalty, pride, and trust.

4. **Developing Leadership that Is Focused on Both Team Development and Team Performance.** Among the special roles that superior team leaders fill are those of initiator, model, and coach.

The "Surveys" portion of the section on Rational/Structured Tools includes an example of a survey tool that teams can use to compare themselves to superior teams.

SECTION 2: RATIONAL/STRUCTURED TOOLS

Rational/structured tools are tools for developing information, making decisions, and solving problems. The tools discussed in this section are brainstorming, the nominal group technique, cause-and-effect diagrams, and flow charts.

Brainstorming

Brainstorming is a group technique for generating information that involves the spontaneous contribution of ideas from all group members. Steps in the brainstorming process typically are:

1. Clarify ground rules for brainstorming.

2. Define topic or information target.
3. Request ideas in sequence from each group member.
4. Follow these rules in generating ideas:

- one idea at a time;
- no criticism or discussion;
- record all ideas, even if they seem repetitious; and
- piggyback on ideas.

5. Record all ideas.
6. End with input in any order from members.
7. Review all ideas and clarify; do not eliminate, only reword as needed.
8. Review all ideas and combine duplicate or similar ideas.
9. Review, clarify, and add to develop final list.

Nominal Group Technique (NGT)

The nominal group technique (NGT) is a highly structured approach to information generation and problem solving. NGT employs a number of sequential steps:

1. A clear definition of the problem or objective of the session;
2. The independent generation of ideas and information by group members;
3. A sequential and objective listing of ideas and information from group members;
4. A discussion and clarification of listed items;
5. Preliminary vote on the importance of each item; and
6. Final vote.

Step 1: Statement of Problem or Objective

NGT focuses the group on a specific problem, question, or objective. Examples are:

- What are the obstacles for improving productivity in our work group?
- What can we do to most dramatically increase productivity in our team or organization?
- Identify ways to measure the quality of our products.

Step 2: Individual Generation of Ideas

The question or problem statement is displayed so that the group has a clear view of it. Each member records his or her own responses to the question.

Cards typically are used to record ideas, one idea to a card. Cards then are collected and used in Step 3.

Step 3: Recording and Displaying Ideas

In the third NGT step, after the cards with members' ideas have been collected, the ideas are recorded on flip charts.

Step 4: Discussion and Clarification

All items are reviewed, and obvious duplications are removed. Items are clarified. The potential usefulness of items is not discussed. Only duplicate items are removed from the list. Items that have been listed are numbered for easy reference in later steps.

Step 5: Preliminary Voting

Independent voting is used to avoid the influences of status, personality, and pressures to conform.

An appropriate number of cards (at least three) is distributed to each member. Members review the list of ideas and select a number of items equivalent to the number of index cards they have been given.

Members then do the following:

1. In the upper left corner of the card, put the number of the item (its number on the posted flip charts).

2. Review each item and select the one from one's cards that is one's first choice; write in the lower right corner of that card the number equivalent to the total number of cards. If eight cards are used, the number for first choice is "8." If five cards are used, the number for first choice is "5," etc.

3. Select the card with the item that is least important or useful for the problem at hand. Write a "1" in the lower right corner.

4. Continue to evaluate all remaining cards in this least-best pattern until all cards are used and the total number of permitted choices has been made.

5. Collect the cards and post the results. The preliminary vote is discussed to identify any strong disagreements and to ensure that everyone has the same information and understanding.

Step 6: Final Vote

A final vote is taken if it is necessary to reduce the list further. The procedure used in Step 5 can be followed, or various weighting techniques can be used.

Cause-and-Effect (CE) Diagram

A CE diagram displays the effect of a process (its quality characteristic or problem) and the causes (or factors) that account for the effect. CE diagrams also are known as fishbone, Ishikawa, or "why?" diagrams.

Steps

Information for the CE Diagram generally is collected by means of a structured process such as brainstorming or the nominal group technique.

1. Select the quality characteristic or problem to be understood, e.g., delay, error, waste, failure. The effect is something that the team wants to improve or control.
2. Write the effect on the right side of the chart. Draw a line from the left side to the "effect."
3. Develop a list of possible causes by using a technique such as brainstorming.
4. Examine the list of causes and see if the causes can be organized into sets or factors. Below the arrow, list the main factors that may be causing the effect. Often the main causes fall into the categories of *materials, work methods, tools, people, or environment (physical and cultural)*.
5. Connect the main factors to the effect line with oblique lines.

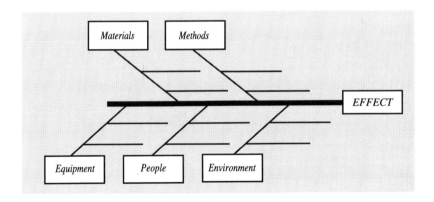

6. Onto each of the main branch items, add the specific factors that may be causes as secondary branches. Onto these secondary branches, add even more specific or discrete

causes, and so on, until all possible causes have been exhausted.

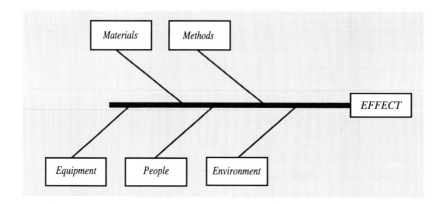

Figure 3-4 (Chapter 3) is an example of a cause-and-effect diagram used for analyzing the possible causes of poor mileage.

Flow Charts

Various symbols are used in flow charts, but in charting work processes, there are a few symbols that have gained general use. They are:

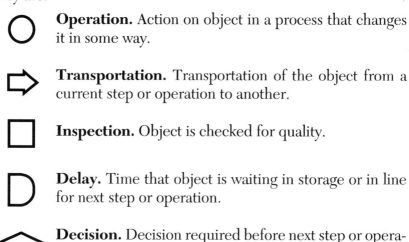

Operation. Action on object in a process that changes it in some way.

Transportation. Transportation of the object from a current step or operation to another.

Inspection. Object is checked for quality.

Delay. Time that object is waiting in storage or in line for next step or operation.

Decision. Decision required before next step or operation in process.

Goals

The goals of flow charting are to:

1. Understand a process;
2. Discover steps that can be eliminated;
3. Discover opportunities to reduce the time it takes to perform each step; and
4. Determine whether the process can be eliminated altogether.

Steps

The sequence for drawing a flow chart is as follows:

1. Select the process to be analyzed.
2. Involve all the people who have knowledge of the process or a major stake in the process in defining it (include operators, customers, and suppliers).
3. Start with the outcome of the process and work backward. Try to identify the major steps first. The data for the process must be charted and made visible to all the people working on the project.
4. Continue to obtain input about the process until each step has been charted.
5. Look for non-valued-added steps (redundancies, unnecessary signatures, inspections, etc.).
6. Look for ways to eliminate all steps that are not operations.
7. Finally, look for ways to reduce the time associated with the performance of any step.

Figures 6-8 and 6-9 (from Chapter 6) are examples of flow charts.

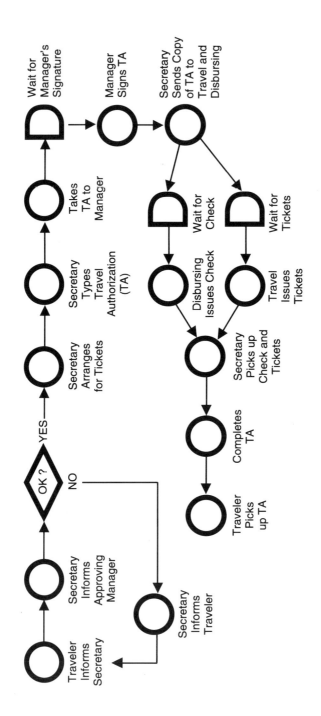

Figure 6-8. Flow Chart of Original Travel-Approval Process

Continuous Improvement and Measurement for Total Quality

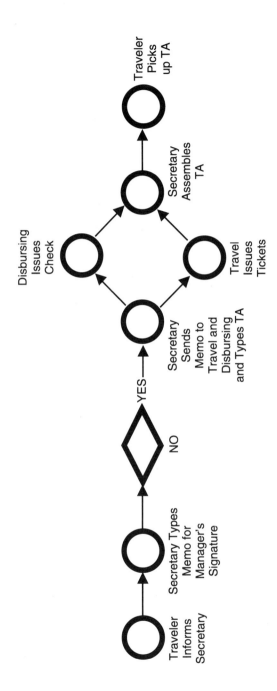

Figure 6-9. Flow Chart of Improved Travel-Approval Process

SECTION 3: NUMERICAL/STATISTICAL TOOLS

Numerical/statistical tools produce or use data that can be displayed as numbers and manipulated statistically. The tools discussed here are surveys, Pareto charts, scatter diagrams, run charts, and control charts.

Surveys

A useful survey must have at least the following characteristics. It must produce:

- data that can be understood,
- data that can be believed, and
- data that can be acted on easily.

In addition to these necessary characteristics, it also is very useful if a survey is simple to administer and easy to analyze.

Surveys can be administered in various ways. Teams can use personal interviews, telephone calls, mailed survey forms, or any combination of these. Data collected can be in the form of ranked responses, rated or scaled responses, or either/or responses.

The surveys and questionnaires used as examples in this Appendix are:

- Superior Team Development Inventory (Kinlaw, 1991)
- Patient Feedback Questionnaire,
- Customer Satisfaction Questionnaire (Engineering Design Group),
- Intergroup Feedback Questionnaire (Kinlaw, 1990), and
- Inquiry Questionnaire.

Survey Example 1

Superior Team Development Inventory (STDI) (Part 4)

Focusing on Leadership

Directions: In completing this part of the *Superior Team Development Inventory,* you must be consistent about the "team" you are rating. The team you are rating consists of you and all the other people who are involved with you as a team in using the inventory.

1. Complete the top section by filling in the blanks with the requested information.
2. Each item in the *STDI* presents a characteristic that may describe your team to some degree or that may not describe your team at all. Indicate the degree to which you believe the item accurately describes your team by circling the appropriate number. "5" indicates that you strongly agree. "1" indicates that you strongly disagree.
3. Complete every item.
4. Follow any special instructions that your team may have established for turning in and scoring your completed survey forms.

THE SUPERVISORS OR LEADERS OF MY TEAM. . .

	Agree				*Disagree*
1. Ensure that the team takes the time it needs to work on its own development.	5	4	3	2	1
2. Make it clear to everyone that team development must be considered part of everyone's job.	5	4	3	2	1

	Agree				Disagree

3. Initiate training to help team members to develop the skills they need to function as a superior team.　　5　4　3　2　1

4. Are quick to acknowledge people who perform as team players.　　5　4　3　2　1

5. Regularly affirm their commitment to team development.　　5　4　3　2　1

6. Take the lead in helping the team to set targets to improve itself as a team.　　5　4　3　2　1

7. Take the lead in having the team evaluate its performance.　　5　4　3　2　1

8. Regularly encourage team members to make full use of one another's competencies.　　5　4　3　2　1

9. Regularly encourage feedback on their performance as team players from other team members.　　5　4　3　2　1

10. Confront other team members positively when these members are not working as team players.　　5　4　3　2　1

11. Are viewed by other members as examples of what team players should be.　　5　4　3　2　1

12. Involve the rest of the team in deciding about new people being brought into the team.　　5　4　3　2　1

		Agree			Disagree	
13.	Make it easy for others to disagree with them.	5	4	3	2	1
14.	Involve the whole team in making decisions that affect the team.	5	4	3	2	1
15.	Always put the team's best interests above their own.	5	4	3	2	1
16.	Always give the team credit for achievements rather than taking credit themselves.	5	4	3	2	1
17.	Lead by gaining the commitment of team members to the team's goals.	5	4	3	2	1
18.	Always encourage team members to resolve their own conflicts with one another before they get involved.	5	4	3	2	1
19.	Ensure that team members are recognized by upper management for their achievements.	5	4	3	2	1
20.	Help other members to participate fully at team meetings.	5	4	3	2	1
21.	Make it easy for others to be candid with them.	5	4	3	2	1
22.	Give their full attention to others when others are speaking.	5	4	3	2	1
23.	Help others to accurately identify problems for themselves.	5	4	3	2	1

	Agree				Disagree
24. Help others take responsibility for solving their own problems.	5	4	3	2	1
25. Provide team members with practical career advice.	5	4	3	2	1
26. Help other members to understand the expectations of senior managers.	5	4	3	2	1
27. Help other team members to identify the knowledge or skills they need to acquire.	5	4	3	2	1
28. Help other team members to gain expert status in their areas of responsibility.	5	4	3	2	1
29. Are very concrete in setting expectations with others about being team players.	5	4	3	2	1
30. Develop concrete strategies with others to improve their performance as team players.	5	4	3	2	1

Survey Example 2

Patient Feedback Questionnaire
(Industrial Medical Facility)

1. Medical Facility Visited:

2. Date Visited:

3. _____Physical Exam _____Treatment _____Other

4. Please rate the following areas. If an "excellent" or "poor" rating is because of an employee's personal service or action, please identify that person by name if possible.

	Excellent	Satisfactory	Poor
Courtesy	___	___	___
Quality of treatment/service	___	___	___
Timeliness	___	___	___
Attitude of personnel	___	___	___
Information/instructions provided	___	___	___
Overall	___	___	___

5. We are continually trying to improve patient care. We solicit your comments/suggestions in the space below.

Please provide the following information if you desire a response to your comments.

Name:

Organization:

Mailing Address:

Survey Example 3

Customer Satisfaction Questionnaire
(Engineering Design Group)

Customer:

Work Package:

Date:

Please circle the number that best describes your level of satisfaction with the following actions or services associated with the work package designated above. A rating of "5" means that you are very satisfied and happy. A rating of "1" means that you are very dissatisfied and unhappy.

	Satisfied			*Dissatisfied*	
1. My level of involvement in planning the design.	5	4	3	2	1
2. Degree to which I have been kept informed about progress with the design.	5	4	3	2	1
3. Degree to which I have been kept informed about planned changes in the design.	5	4	3	2	1
4. Technical correctness and accuracy of the design.	5	4	3	2	1
5. Completeness of design package.	5	4	3	2	1
6. Planning schedule for design production.	5	4	3	2	1
7. Management of design schedule.	5	4	3	2	1

	Satisfied				Dissatisfied

8. Expenditure of hours (engineering and drafting) on design. 5 4 3 2 1

9. Cooperation with me by
   engineering design department. 5 4 3 2 1

10. Please make any comments below that could help us in any
    way to assure that you are, become, or stay *very* satisfied with
    our services to you.

Survey Example 4

Intergroup Feedback Questionnaire (IFQ)
by Dennis C. Kinlaw, Ed.D.

The *IFQ* has been designed to give managers, supervisors, and
members of a work group a tool with which to:

1. Assess the perceptions of their group's characteristics and
   performance by members of another work group, and
2. Identify specific targets to improve the way in which their
   group works with the other group.

Work group being described:

Work group filling out survey:

Date:

Directions: Each item in the *IFQ* describes a characteristic of
another work group with which your work group interacts or does
business. On the survey form, indicate the degree to which you

believe each statement accurately describes the other work group. Do this by circling the appropriate number. Please respond to every item in the survey.

"5" indicates that you **strongly agree** with the statement.
"1" indicates that you **do not agree at all** with the statement.

THE OTHER WORK GROUP TYPICALLY...

	Agree				*Disagree*
1. Clarifies for us what it routinely expects from us.	5	4	3	2	1
2. Regularly gives us timely feedback on the work we do with/for it.	5	4	3	2	1
3. Keeps us aware of its priorities that affect us.	5	4	3	2	1
4. Clarifies for us the standards it uses to judge the work we do with/for it.	5	4	3	2	1
5. Regularly keeps us aware of changes in policy or practices that affect how we work together —before these changes are implemented.	5	4	3	2	1
6. Gives us easy access to the people we need to contact.	5	4	3	2	1
7. Gives us prompt help on priority problems.	5	4	3	2	1
8. Carries its fair share of the work for which we have shared responsibility.	5	4	3	2	1

	Agree				Disagree
9. Gives us a prompt decision when we need it.	5	4	3	2	1
10. Is quite helpful in working with our group to adjust schedules to meet unforeseen events.	5	4	3	2	1
11. Does sufficient joint planning with our group.	5	4	3	2	1
12. Rarely gives us a priority that was created by its own poor planning or lack of foresight.	5	4	3	2	1
13. Maintains efficient work-flow processes between our groups.	5	4	3	2	1
14. Rarely causes our group to redo tasks or assignments that could have been avoided.	5	4	3	2	1
15. Maintains effective reporting procedures between our groups.	5	4	3	2	1
16. Makes good use of our group's expertise.	5	4	3	2	1
17. Is good about sharing its equipment with us to help us do our best work.	5	4	3	2	1
18. Gives us the time we need to do our best work.	5	4	3	2	1
19. Ensures that we have the information we need to do our best work.	5	4	3	2	1

		Agree				Disagree

20. Dedicates time to focus with us on how to improve the way our groups work together. 5 4 3 2 1

21. Shares with us a strong commitment to common goals. 5 4 3 2 1

22. Can be counted on to meet the commitments it makes to our group. 5 4 3 2 1

23. Is more interested in solving problems than in assigning blame. 5 4 3 2 1

24. Has more interest in getting the job done than "in protecting its turf." 5 4 3 2 1

25. Does a good job of encouraging our group to make decisions that are appropriate for it to make. 5 4 3 2 1

26. Takes responsibility for its own failures. 5 4 3 2 1

27. Is good about giving our group credit for the successes to which we contribute. 5 4 3 2 1

28. Is quick to express appreciation when our group makes a special effort to respond to its requests. 5 4 3 2 1

29. Gives serious consideration to our group's suggestions on how to improve the way we work together. 5 4 3 2 1

30. Does not waste our group's time. 5 4 3 2 1

	Agree				Disagree
31. Uses the appropriate contact person in our work group.	5	4	3	2	1
32. Makes it clear who the appropriate contact persons are in it.	5	4	3	2	1
33. Demonstrates that it is clear about its own responsibilities in working with our group.	5	4	3	2	1
34. Demonstrates that it is clear about the responsibilities of our group in working with it.	5	4	3	2	1
35. Has a clearly defined, internal organizational structure.	5	4	3	2	1
36. Is quick to identify to our group any areas of conflict that it experiences.	5	4	3	2	1
37. Makes it easy for our group to identify (for it) any areas of conflict that our group experiences.	5	4	3	2	1
38. Tries to reach "win/win" or positive resolutions of conflicts with our group when conflicts occur.	5	4	3	2	1
39. Treats conflicts with our group as a potentially useful way to improve the way we work together.	5	4	3	2	1
40. Avoids unnecessary conflict by straight and open communication with no "hidden agendas."	5	4	3	2	1

Survey Example 5

Inquiry Questionnaire

1. If you were to raise a question with your immediate supervisor (or any other person senior to you in your organization) about the usefulness, efficiency, or effectiveness of some aspect of the way in which work or business is conducted, you would expect that (*check one*):

a___ Your question would be given **full** consideration.

b___ Your question would be given **some** consideration.

c___ Your question would be given **little or no** consideration.

2. If you were to make a specific suggestion to your immediate supervisor (or any other person senior to you in your organization) about how to improve some aspect of your job, you would expect that (*check one*):

a___ If you demonstrated the improvement potential of the suggestion, it would be given **full** consideration.

b___ If you demonstrated the improvement potential of the suggestion, it would be given **some** consideration.

c___ Even if you demonstrated the improvement potential of the suggestion, it would be given **little or no** consideration.

3. Indicate how often improvements are made in the ways in which you and your closest coworkers perform any aspect of your work (*check one*):

a___ Very often

b___ Occasionally

c___ Almost never

4. How frequently do you have new ideas about how to improve some aspect of the way in which your job is performed (*check one*)?

a___ At least once a week

b___ At least once a month

c___ Less often than once a month

5. How frequently over the past year have you **actually presented** ideas to your supervisor (or any other person senior to you in your organization) to improve some aspect of the way in which work or business is conducted (*check one*)?

a___ At least once a week

b___ At least once a month

c___ Less frequently than once a month

6. How typical has it been that, when you have **actually presented** ideas to your supervisor (or any other person senior to you in your organization) to improve some aspect of the way in which work or business is conducted, that some **concrete action** resulted from your ideas (*check one*)?

a___ Very typical

b___ Somewhat typical

c___ Not very typical at all

Pareto Charts

The sequence for constructing a Pareto chart is:

1. Select the data that will be retrieved, e.g., kinds of accidents occurring, kinds of errors made, areas of customer dissatisfaction.

2. Decide how the data will be categorized or summarized, e.g., by location of error, by time of error, by worker, by machine.

3. Design or select the tally sheet to be used.

4. Make observations and complete the tally sheet.

5. Make a bar graph by arranging the categorized data in descending order of frequency. Divide the horizontal axis into the number of bars required for the number of categories used. Use vertical axes to measure number of observations in each category (bar).

6. Draw a cumulative curve showing how much each bar contributes to the total (100 percent) of all observations.

Figure 6-14 (in Chapter 6) is an example of a Pareto Diagram.

Histograms

The steps in preparing a histogram are as follows:

1. Decide on the kinds, number, and period of observations.

2. Tally the observations.

   For example, suppose that Figure A-1 is a tally of the observations of the time it took to complete the paperwork for a small-dollar procurement request in the Timewarp Space Systems Company.

3. Identify the greatest and smallest values in the observations. In the example: greatest value= 4.10 hours; smallest value= 2.45 hours.

Observations (Measured in Hours)					Smallest	Greatest
3.56	3.26	2.45	2.55	3.30	2.45	3.56
2.55	3.60	3.75	3.80	2.90	2.55	3.80
3.60	3.78	3.50	4.00	3.20	3.20	4.00
3.45	2.78	3.49	3.60	2.90	2.78	3.60
2.80	3.48	3.58	2.88	4.10	2.80	4.10

Figure A-1. Time To Complete Procurement Request

4. Determine the range between the greatest and smallest observations. In the example, it is 4.10 less 2.45 = range of 1.65 hours.

5. Determine the number of classes (number of bars). If there are 100 observations or less, we can start with ten classes. If there are more than 100 observations, we should begin to increase our classes, but it usually is convenient to start with ten.

6. Determine the width of classes. In the example: Class interval = Range/number of classes = 1.65/10 = .165. For convenience, express the class interval as a multiple of an integer. In this case, we can use 0.20.

7. Determine class boundaries. We do not want any of our observations to fall on a class boundary. We want our observations to fall within boundaries so that we know to which class they belong. There are a number of ways to accomplish this; one way is as follows. The observations have values such as 3.56, 3.30, 2.90, etc. The smallest unit of measure that we have used is 0.01. Make the boundary unit *half* of the actual units of measurement. In the example that we are using, one half of the measurement unit is 0.5 x 0.01 = .005. Subtract .005 from the lowest amount of the lowest observation. 2.45 less .005 is 2.445. Thereby, 2.445

becomes our lowest class boundary. We then create our classes or bars by adding the class interval of 0.2 to the lowest boundary and then 0.2 to that sum and so on until ten classes are created.

8. Tally observations by class. For example:

2.445 to 2.645	(3)
2.645 to 2.845	(2)
2.845 to 3.045	(3)
3.045 to 3.245	(1)
3.245 to 3.445	(2)
3.445 to 3.645	(9)
3.645 to 3.845	(3)
3.845 to 4.045	(1)
4.045 to 4.245	(1)

9. Create the histogram.

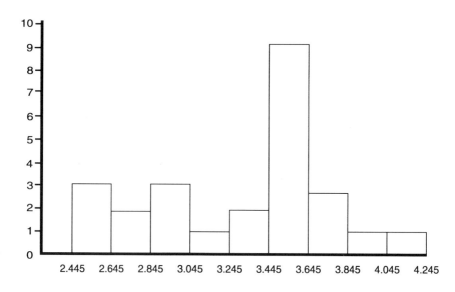

Run Charts

Run charts can help teams to identify opportunities and problems by tracking such things as:

- defects occurring per unit,
- days of sick leave taken per organization,
- amount of scrap produced,
- errors in cashing checks per banking day,
- errors in medication per shift, and so on.

Run charts can tell a team whether the process is performing as expected and whether it is tending to get better or worse. Run charts are prepared as follows:

1. Select a quality indicator to track;
2. Select units of measurement for the quality indicator and place these units in ascending order on the vertical axis;
3. Select equal time intervals and place these on the horizontal axis; and
4. Make and record observations.

Examples of run charts are found in Figures 4-8 and 4-9 (Chapter 4).

Scatter Diagrams

A scatter diagram is used to display the possible relationship of one variable to another, e.g., training to demonstrated competence in a skill, errors in time cards to time submitted, or stability of a compound to shelf time.

A scatter diagram shows the degree of positive or negative correlation that might exist between two variables. Diagram A shows a positive correlation. As x increases, y increases. Diagram B shows a negative correlation. As x increases, y decreases. Diagram C shows no apparent correlation between x and y.

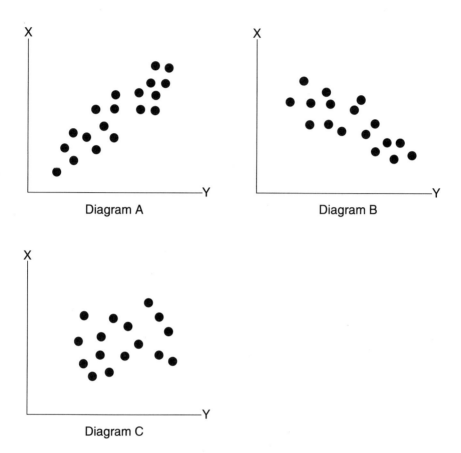

Diagram A

Diagram B

Diagram C

The steps in making a scatter diagram are:

1. Select the two variables that you want to examine for a possible correlation.

2. Draw the x and y axes for the diagram and select an appropriate measure and scale to use. Make the values higher as you move upward along the x axis and to the right along the y axis.

3. Collect and plot the data.

Control Charts

The basis for the construction and use of control charts is as follows:

- Any set of measurements that varies will form a distribution.

- Any such distribution will have an average, and its variation can be measured by statistics such as range or standard deviation.

- Unless the distribution is badly distorted, very few points will fall outside the band of plus or minus three standard deviations from the distribution's average *due to chance causes alone.*

The number that represents plus three standard deviations is called the *upper control limit.* The number that represents minus three standard deviations from the mean is called the *lower control limit.* We can conclude that any measurement within the upper and lower control limits is *general*, and its cause is attributable to chance alone. We also can conclude that any measurement outside the control limits is *special* and has an assignable cause.

To use control charts, we must be able to understand, compute, and use control limits. Control limits are computed from the estimated variability of a process and typically mean plus or minus three standard deviations above or below the performance average of a process. When a process is behaving normally and is free from errors that are caused by special causes, 99.7 percent of all measurements will fall within plus or minus three standard deviations from the average.

Estimates of the standard deviations of a process are computed in various ways—depending on the kind of data involved and the kind of control chart that is being constructed. In Chapter 6, an example for computing control limits and standard deviations for $\overline{X}R$ charts is given.

Control charts are developed to enable us to understand, control, or improve any of a number of statistics that tell us how a process is performing. The kind of data that is collected determines the kind of chart that is used. If we are counting something such as the number of errors or defects, we are using *attribute* data. If we are collecting data about length, time, weight, resistance, or torque, we are using *measurement* data.

There are a number of control charts that can be used for each kind of data. The charts that are in most common use are defined as follows.

Control charts that can be used when we count the number of something, i.e. attribute data, are:

- **c Charts.** These are charts of the number of errors in collected samples in which the size of the samples stays the same, e.g., errors on an exam in samples of twenty students, mistakes in measuring blood pressures of fifty patients, etc.

- **u Charts.** These are similar to c charts, but the size of the comparison group does not remain the same, and an adjustment is made to permit comparisons. To use the example of errors per student, one sample may have twenty students and other samples may range from ten to fifty. All observations of different-sized samples are converted to the base of fifty. For example, a sample size of twenty is 20/50 or .40 of the base. Suppose ten errors were observed in this sample. Ten errors in the sample of twenty would translate into 10/.40, or a "unitized" error count of 25. It is this unitized count that is used in the u chart.

- **pn and p Charts.** These charts plot proportions computed from ratios such as the number of acceptable fasteners per number inspected, the number of medication errors per twenty-five patients, the number of items missed on a test per fifty students, etc. The p chart is used with sample sizes that vary. A pn chart is used with samples of constant size.

The two charts most commonly used for continuous measurement data are:

- **X̄R Charts.** X̄R charts measure how the *means and ranges* of a process vary. By plotting the means of sample data, we can determine how stable these means are, i.e., is the measurement that we are tracking getting larger or smaller or staying about the same? By plotting the range, we can tell if the amount of spread around the mean is becoming greater or smaller, i.e., is there more or less variation in the measurements of the product being produced?

- $\overline{X}S$ **Charts.** $\overline{X}S$ charts measure how the *means and standard deviations* of a process vary. They perform the same function as $\overline{X}R$ charts, only the amount of variation is tracked by using the standard deviation.

Type of Data	Chart Name
Discrete or counting data	c Chart (number of defects) u Chart (defects per unit) pn Chart (number of defective units) p Chart (percentage defective)
Continuous or measurement data	$\overline{X}R$ **Charts** (average and range of samples) $\overline{X}S$ **Charts** (average and standard deviations of samples)

Types of Control Charts

The reader may refer to the "References" at the end of this book for further sources of help in understanding and constructing control charts.

SECTION 4: RECORD-KEEPING AND TRACKING TOOLS

As teams plan and implement improvement projects, they may employ a wide variety of tools to keep track of what they are doing, how well they are doing, who has what responsibilities, and when they reach milestones. The following are examples of two such record-keeping and tracking tools.

Improvement target: Project lead: Date begun: Date Completed:				
Planned Actions	Start Date	End Date	Responsibility	Notes

Project-Management Form

The next example shows the milestones for improving a process, which we will name "X." The open triangles show milestones planned but not completed. The solid triangles show milestones that have been reached. Triangles that are joined indicate milestones that begin in one month and are completed in another.

Improvement-Project Milestones

Event/Action	1/92	2/92	3/92	4/92	5/92	6/92	7/92
Identify process	▲						
Select project team	▲						
Create flow chart of process	▲—▲						
Identify opportunities		▲—▲					
Develop plan			▲—△				
Implement plan				△			
Begin tracking data				△			
Begin statusing					△		

Date: 4/1/92

References

Argyris, C. (1988). *Reasoning, learning and action.* San Francisco: Jossey-Bass.

Argyris, C. (1990). *Overcoming organizational defenses.* New York: Prentice-Hall.

Argyris, C., & Schon, D. (1978). *Organizational learning: A theory of action perspective.* Reading, MA: Addison-Wesley.

Baldrige competition keeps suppliers competitive. (1989, October). *Technowledge,* p. 3.

Beacon Press, Inc. (1989). *How grocery buyers rate the various food chains in metropolitan Richmond.* Richmond, VA: Author.

Boothe, R. (1990, February). Who defines quality in service industries? *Quality Progress,* pp. 65-67.

Buffa, E.S. (1984). *Meeting the competitive challenge.* Homewood, IL: Dow Jones-Irwin.

Burr, I.W. (1976). *Statistical quality control methods.* New York: Marcel Dekker.

Campbell, D. (1985). *Take the road to creativity and get off your dead end.* Greensboro, NC: Center for Creative Leadership.

Crosby, P.B. (1979). *Quality is free.* New York: McGraw-Hill.

Crosby, P.B. (1984). *Quality without tears.* New York: McGraw-Hill.

de Geus, A. (1988, March-April). Planning as learning. *Harvard Business Review,* pp. 70-74.

Deming, W.E. (1981). *Japanese methods for productivity and quality.* Washington, DC: George Washington University.

Deming, W.E. (1982). *Quality, productivity, and competitive position.* Cambridge, MA: Massachusetts Institute of Technology.

Deming, W.E. (1985). *Out of the crisis.* Cambridge, MA: Massachusetts Institute of Technology.

Drucker, P.F. (1974). *Management.* New York: Harper & Row.

Feigenbaum, A.V. (1983). *Total quality control.* New York: McGraw-Hill.

Fitzgibbons, R.G., & Juran, J.M. (1974). Vendor relations. In J.M. Juran (Ed.), *Quality control handbook.* New York: McGraw-Hill.

Halberstam, D. (1986). *The reckoning.* New York: William Morrow.

Hammer, M. (1990, July-August). Reengineering work: Don't automate, obliterate. *Harvard Business Review,* pp. 104-112.

Harvey, J.B. (1988). *The Abilene paradox and other meditations on management.* Lexington, MA: Lexington Books/San Diego, CA: Pfeiffer & Company.

Ishikawa, K. (1985). *What is total quality control? The Japanese way.* Englewood Cliffs, NJ: Prentice-Hall.

Jewell, R., & Airey, C. (1984). *British social attitudes: The 1984 report.* Aldershot, England: Gower.

Juran, J.M. (1964). *Managerial breakthrough.* New York: McGraw-Hill.

Juran, J.M. (1986, August). The quality trilogy. *Quality Progress.*

Kilmann, R.H. (1984). *Beyond the quick fix.* San Francisco: Jossey-Bass.

Kinlaw, D.C. (1989). *Coaching for commitment: Managerial strategies for obtaining superior performance.* San Diego, CA: Pfeiffer & Company.

Kinlaw, D.C. (1990). *Inter-group feedback questionnaire.* Norfolk, VA: Kinlaw Associates.

Kinlaw, D.C. (1991). *Developing superior work teams: Building quality and the competitive edge.* Lexington, MA: Lexington Books/San Diego, CA: Pfeiffer & Company.

Kinlaw, D.C. (1991). *Superior team development inventory.* Norfolk, VA: Kinlaw Associates.

Kirkpatrick, D.L. (1985). *How to manage change effectively.* San Francisco: Jossey-Bass.

Lindblom, C.B. (1990). *Inquiry and change.* New Haven, CT: Yale University Press.

Lippitt, G.L., Langseth, P., & Mossop, J. (1985). *Implementing organizational change.* San Francisco: Jossey-Bass.

McDonald, J.E., Jr., & James, E. (1987, Winter). The sweet smell of success. *Powerline,* pp. 19-25.

Manufacturing the right way. (1990, May 21). *Fortune,* pp. 54-72.

Michael, S.R. (1981). *Techniques of organizational change.* New York: McGraw-Hill.

Montgomery, D.C. (1985). *Introduction to statistical quality control.* New York: John Wiley.

Osborn, A.F. (1979). *Applied imagination: Principles and procedures of creative problem-solving* (3rd. rev. ed.). New York: Charles Scribner's. [Orig. ed. 1953.]

Ott, E.R. (1975). *Process quality control.* New York: McGraw-Hill.

Ritti, R.R., & Funkhouser, G.R. (1982). *The ropes to skip and the ropes to know.* Columbus, OH: Grid.

Rokeach, M. (1960). *The open and closed mind.* New York: Basic Books.

Schulman, D.H., & Salvolaine, C.G. (1990). AT&T's competitive advantage—Quality of service. *AT&T Technology, 5*(2), 4-8.

Senge, P.M. (1990). *The fifth discipline: The art and practice of the learning organization.* New York: Doubleday.

Shewhart, W.A. (1931). *The economic control of quality of manufactured product.* New York: Van Nostrand. [Reprinted in 1981 by the American Society for Quality Control.]

Siegel, J. (1966, July). A practical approach to vendor ratings. *Industrial Quality Control,* pp. 17-19.

Sink, D.S. (1985). *Productivity management: Planning, measurement and evaluation, control and improvement.* New York: John Wiley.

Spence, L. (1978). *The politics of social knowledge.* University Park, PA: Pennsylvania State University Press.

Stata, R. (1989, Spring). Organizational learning—The key to management innovation. *Sloan Management Review,* pp. 63-64.

Taylor, C.W. (Ed.). (1964). *Creativity: Progress and potential.* New York: McGraw-Hill.

Tichy, N.M. (1983). *Managing strategic change.* New York: John Wiley.

Tuttle, T.C., & Romanowski, J.J. (1985, Summer). Assessing performance and productivity in white-collar organizations. *National Productivity Review, 4*(3), 211-224.

Twiss, B.C. (1986). *Managing technological innovation.* New York: Longman.

van Grundy, A.B. (1985). *Techniques of structured problem solving.* New York: Van Nostrand Reinhold.

Verba, S., & Orren, G.R. (1985). *Equality in America.* Cambridge, MA: Harvard University Press.

Wheeler, D.J., & Chambers, D.S. (1986). *Understanding statistical process and control.* Knoxville, TN: Statistical Process Controls.

Yankelovich, D., & Immerwahr, J. (1983). *Putting the work ethic to work.* New York: The Public Agenda Foundation.

Index

F

Feigenbaum, A.V., viii
Fitzgibbons, R.G., 173
Flow chart, 4, 46, 48, 65, 145, 211
Fortune, 165, 184
Funkhouser, G.R., 180

G

Grundy, A.B., 48

H

Halberstam, D., 193
Hammer, M., 185
Harvey, J.B., 179
Histogram, 2, 4, 46, 56, 145, 232

I

Immerwahr, J., 12
Improvement, 7, 10, 12, 16-17, 19, 21-22, 24, 36, 41-42, 64, 89, 122, 132, 153, 159, 161, 177, 181, 190, 197, 199
Improvement projects, ix, 4, 24-25, 40- 44, 63, 66, 70, 74-75, 106, 111, 131, 144, 167-168, 239
Input, 21, 24, 34, 39, 131, 159, 162, 167-168, 170
Inquiry, 177, 179, 185, 189, 191, 196, 200, 229
Ishikawa, K., viii, 45

J

James, E., 101
Jewell, R., 179
JIT, 38, 184
Juran, J.M., vii-viii, 173

K

Kinlaw, D.C., 1, 5, 26, 31, 39, 46, 65, 66, 75, 77, 82-83, 182, 205, 218, 224
Kirkpatrick, D.L., 198

L

Lindblom, C.B., 179
Lippitt, G.L., 198

M

Malcolm Baldrige Award, 163
McDonald, J.E., 101
Michael, S.R., 198
Montgomery, D.C., 45, 59
Morrison, Inc., 117

N

NASA, 107, 161, 164-165, 167
Nominal group technique, 48, 107, 168, 208

O

Operations, 130
    relationship of processes and, 33

as supplier, 21, 39
Team development, viii, 19,
24-25, 30, 39, 47, 75-76,
161, 167, 218
Team meeting evaluation
sheet, 88
Team meetings, 83, 189, 202
Team members, 17, 26, 106,
169
Team-centered total quality
management, 1, 4, 76, 165
Team-member feedback, 87
Teams, 20
Tichy, N.M., 198
Total Quality Management,
vii, 1, 44, 86, 177, 182
Total Quality Management
Tools, 5, 44, 205
models, 46, 205
numerical/statistical, 46, 50,
215
structured/rational, 46, 48,
207
Toyota, 38, 184

Training, 2, 195
Tuttle, T.C., 112
Twiss, B.C., 179

U
Ukrop's Super Markets, 100

V
Values, 179-181, 183, 200
Variation, 68, 132, 135-137,
237
Verba, S., 188

W
Wheeler, D.J., 45, 59

X
XR chart, 238

Y
Yankelovich, D., 12

Z
Zenger/Miller, 28

Editor: Arlette C. Ballew
Editorial Assistance: Steffany N. Perry
Jennifer Bryant
Cover Design: Heather Kennedy
Graphic Artist: Heather Kennedy
Page Compositor: Judy Whalen

This book was edited and formatted using 386 platforms with 8MB RAM and high-resolution, dual-page monitors. The copy was produced using WordPerfect software; pages composed with Ventura software; illustrations produced in Corel Draw or hand drawn. The text is set in twelve on fourteen New Caledonia, and heads are Helvetica Ultra Compressed and New Caledonia Italic. Camera-ready copy was output on a 1200-dpi laser imagesetter by Pfeiffer & Company.